W9-COG-158

Praise for *Generation Fix*

"*A skilled journalist whose respect for young people shines through, Elizabeth Rusch tells remarkable stories of children who accomplish extraordinary things to make this a better world. [Generation Fix] is essential reading for children who know almost instinctively what their communities need—and for parents and teachers who want to support young people's natural inclination to make a difference in the lives of others.*"
—Senator Edward M. Kennedy

"*Read this book and you will never underestimate the power of the next generation, which Rusch rightly calls Generation Fix.*"
—Ronald Wolk, *Teacher Magazine*

"*At last—a book about teens that will motivate people of all ages to improve our world. This should be required reading for anyone working with young people.*"
—Suzanne Barchers, *Read magazine/Weekly Reader*

"*This isn't just another book about do-gooders. This is about kids who saw problems...and solved them. Prepare to be inspired!*"
—Betsy Kohn, *Guideposts for Teens*

"*Upbeat snapshots of students of all ages who make a difference in their communities. Maybe these young people are not changing the world, but they are changing their world, and that's a significant story for our times.*"
—Christopher Broderick, *The Oregonian*

"*Rusch proves, in a clever and approachable way, that today's kids are finding creative solutions to problems that have stumped generations. Start small, dream big, save the world—what better lesson to learn from our children?*"
—Eric Elkins, *Denver Post* and *Rocky Mountain News*

"*A fantastic resource for teachers who care about the planet and want to invite kids to have a voice in how the world works and to write for real reasons. I can't wait to show it to my students.*"
—Nancie Atwell, middle-school teacher
and author of *In the Middle*

GENERATION FIX

Young Ideas
for a Better World

Elizabeth Rusch

BEYOND
WORDS
Publishing
I N C

To Craig and Cobi

Published by
Beyond Words Publishing, Inc.
20827 NW Cornell Road, Suite 500
Hillsboro, Oregon 97124
(503) 531-8700/ (800) 284-9673

Copyright © 2002 by Elizabeth Rusch
Illustrations Copyright © 2002 by Pamela Hobbs

Cover and interior design by:Amy Arendts
Proofread by David Abel

All rights reserved. No part of this book may be reproduced or transmitted in any form or by any means, electronic or mechanical, including photocopying, recording, or by any informa-tion storage or retrieval system, without the written permission of Beyond Words Publishing, Inc., except where permitted by law. This book contains stories about real kids dealing with real situations. Beyond Words Publishing, Inc. recommends that parents review the contents of this book for younger or more sensitive readers.

Printed in the United States of America
Distributed to the book trade by Publishers Group West

Every effort has been made to contact the copyright owners of the photographs and illustra-tions in this book. If the copyright holder of a photograph or illustration in this book has not heard from us, please contact Beyond Words Publishing. The publisher gratefully acknowl-edges and thanks the following for generous assistance and permission to use photos:

Charlie and Davon King, photo by David Dalton; April Mathews and Kerri Stephen, photo courtesy of J.C. Penny Company, Inc., Dusty Hill cover photo by Nancy Hill, Ann Lai; courtesy of Stiftung Jugend forscht e.V. / Deutsche Bank AG, Gabriella Contreras cover photo by Bruce McClelland, Arizona Daily Star; Hannah Jukovsky photo copyright © 2001 by Linda Haas, Sol Kelley-Jones, photo by John Quinlan, Ryan Tripp cover photo, courtesy of The Office of the Governor, Alaska; and Jason Crowe photo copyright © 1999 by Barton Wilder Custom Images #5964-27, author photo by Dani Swope.

ISBN: 1-58270-067-2

Library of Congress Cataloging-in-Publication Data

Rusch, Elizabeth.
    Generation Fix: Young ideas for a better world / written by Elizabeth Rusch ; illustrated by Pamela Hobbs.
        p. cm.
    Summary: Features the true stories of more than twenty young activists doing things to make the world a better place.
    ISBN 1-58270-067-2 (softcover)
        1. Voluntarism—Case Studies—Juvenile literature. 2. Social action—Case stud-ies—Juvenile literature. 3. Social advocacy—Case Studies—Juvenile literature. 4. Young volunteers—Case Studies—Juvenile literature. [1. Voluntarism. 2. Volunteers in social service.] I. Hobbs, Pamela, ill. II. Title.

HN49.V64 R87 2002
361.2—dc21
2001058952

The corporate mission of Beyond Words Publishing, Inc:
Inspire to Integrity.

TABLE OF CONTENTS

Are You Part of Generation Fix?

"The future belongs to those who believe in the beauty of their dreams." —Eleanor Roosevelt

*T*wenty million people die of starvation every year. Millions are homeless. More than a *billion* people in the world have no access to a doctor. For centuries, adults have struggled to solve these problems. I think the solutions will come from you, the next generation—Generation Fix.

I discovered Generation Fix while interviewing kids for my column "KidSpeak" in *Child* magazine. One day I asked kids: "What do you think we should do about pollution?" Total silence. "Maybe kids don't care," I thought, "or they don't have any ideas." I was wrong. The kids were thinking—hard. They took the question really seriously and came up with remarkable, creative answers.

After years of interviewing, I felt I had finally heard the true voice of your generation. I learned that you know and care about the serious problems we face in the world and are trying to make a difference. Your generation has ideas—some simple ideas, some complex ideas, and some ideas that might sound crazy, but just might work. The world needs to hear what you think, and learn about how you are already making the world better. That's what this book is all about.

Each chapter in this book tells the stories of kids who saw a problem and did something about it. You'll find out how kids just like you tackled hunger, homelessness, violence, discrimination, and problems with health care, education, and the environment. It was tough to choose whose stories to include—there were so many!

The kids in this book are ordinary—but their achievements are extraordinary. They have collected more than 5,000 boxes of cereal for food pantries, recycled 30,000 gallons of oil, raised a quarter of a million dollars to buy school supplies for needy kids, invented a sensor to better control acid rain, and marched with picket signs to stop violence. One even rode a lawnmower clear across the country to raise awareness about organ donation.

You've probably heard that problems can spiral out of control. In this book you'll read about *solutions* that spiraled out of control. In the first year of Breakfast Bonanza, Zachary Ebers collected an astonishing 800 boxes of cereal for the hungry. "I was just doing what I could to help," he says. "I didn't know how successful we would be. It was kind of amazing."

Their work was never easy. Josh Marcus had to overcome the urge to play basketball when backpacks needed to be stuffed with school supplies. Kristel Fritz struggled to convince appearance-conscious teenagers to donate their hair. Kate Klinkerman's first attempt to keep oil from contaminating groundwater actually made the problem worse.

These kids are not perfect. They are not saints. They are not geniuses. But they represent a generation with the energy and ideas needed to fix our broken world.

Ideas from Generation Fix

Sprinkled throughout this book are smart, funny, and dead-serious solutions to world problems from kids all over the country. When I asked kids like you for their ideas, some so overflowed with suggestions that I could barely write fast enough. Others were skeptical, slumping back in their chairs, arms crossed. No one had ever asked them what should be done about homelessness, hunger, or health care. Eventually, they spoke, leaning forward, gesturing. In the end, every kid I interviewed offered an idea that made me think. Made me wonder. Made me hope.

Many proposed gun control, universal health insurance, curbside recycling, and smaller class sizes. But instead of picking these common suggestions, I chose the most quirky, creative ideas. After all, a hundred years ago, who would have believed that we'd have flying machines, cars powered by the sun, and medicines made from viruses?

Our Future

Many people say that kids are our future. Some people mean that the world will be better when you grow up and run our schools, governments, families, and businesses. I know we don't have to wait that long. Generation Fix can bring us a better world right now.

—Elizabeth Rusch

Chapter One

YOU KNOW SCHOOL

"Learning is wealth that can't be stolen."—**Philippine proverb**

It's 10:00 AM on a weekday and you sit at your desk, your pen poised over a sheet of paper. The pen moves, first in a round twirling motion, then in jagged little scratches. You sketch out a smiling face and add shaggy hair, glasses, and a moustache. You are not in art class, yet your aimless drawing continues—you are doodling. Believe it or not, someone has measured the distance that an average sixth grader doodles during the school year: 1.3 miles!

You have time for miles of doodling because you spend so many hours in school—an average of 16,000 hours by the time you will graduate high school. That makes you a true expert when it comes to education and the school scene. You know what works and what doesn't. Yet no one asks you how to make school more interesting, how to help you learn more.

Until now, that is: a polling group called Public Agenda asked 1,200 kids what they thought of education and how to improve it. Here's what you said:

Do you always want the easy way out?

No way, according to this study. Half of students say that school is not tough enough. Seven out of ten kids say they would pay more attention to their schoolwork and actually learn more if teachers expected more of them.

"I think they don't take us seriously enough," said one teen. "We're really smarter than they think. It's how far and how they push us."

Kids were even asked to choose between a fun teacher who demands hard work or a boring teacher who is easy. The tough teacher won hands down, with eight in ten kids voting that way.

Are your textbooks old? Your classes crowded?

Your schools crumbling? Schools need more money for books and computers, and to fix old buildings, kids say. Other studies show that kids are right. One in three schools needs massive repairs or replacement, according to a study by the U.S. General Accounting Office. Yet the federal government spends four times as much money each day on a prison inmate as it spends on a public school student.

Do you want to do well in school?

You want to learn and do well in school and you admire classmates who get good grades. In fact, almost all kids say doing well in school makes them feel really good about themselves.

Kids like you have tons of ideas for improving schools and education. Here are the stories of some who are taking action to make it happen.

Sack it to You!

Joshua Marcus

"When I handed the kids backpacks, they were so happy. It was such a good feeling, I couldn't stop." —Joshua Marcus

A month before Josh Marcus turned 10, the principal at Josh's school in Boca Raton, Florida, announced that all students would be required to do community service. They could work at soup kitchens, homeless shelters, or clean up beaches, the principal suggested. "I didn't want to be like everybody else," Josh says. "I wanted to be me." And that meant finding a problem and creating his own solution.

"I asked my mom to take me to Miami where poor people lived so I could help," he says. "I thought Boca Raton was this fairy-tale place with no poverty."

But needy people live all over the world, even in Boca

Raton, his mom said. And she showed Josh by taking him to Florence Fuller Child Development Center, a day-care center in a neighborhood of migrant farm workers.

Josh offered to help teach the young children. No go. The director told him he had to be at least 16 years old to work with kids. "Well, is there anything the kids need?" he asked. School supplies for when they start kindergarten, the director said.

Josh was shocked that some families couldn't afford the basic tools of learning: paper, pencils, notebooks, and rulers. Josh promised that the 152 kids starting kindergarten in the fall would have all the supplies they would need, packed in their very own brand new backpack.

Sack It To You! was born. Josh designed a logo and made business cards and stationery on his computer. Every day after school, he asked stores that sold backpacks or school supplies for donations. Day after day he was turned down.

He decided to try another approach. Maybe he could raise money to buy the packs and supplies. To raise the $7,600 he needed, Josh mailed out letters to family, friends, his parents' friends, and businesses, asking for donations. He also knocked on doors in his neighborhood. At the end of the summer, armed with the donations and a list, he went shopping. "When I handed the kids backpacks, they were so happy," Josh says. "It was such a good feeling, I couldn't stop."

Neglected Teens, Needed Supplies

Josh read in the paper that the Haven, a home for abused and neglected teens, needed school supplies. Josh took care of it. He raised another $6,400 for 128 packs. "When I gave these big macho kids backpacks—something I always took for granted—some of them broke down and cried," he says.

To Josh's surprise, reporters started calling. "I thought community service was something that no one really cared about," he says. "I thought you could only get on the news if you did something like kill somebody."

The attention brought more donations. Office Depot offered to reimburse Josh for all the supplies for every backpack he donated. (Later, because of budget cuts, they covered only supplies Josh couldn't afford, and then switched to providing thousands of backpacks, some filled with supplies.) And the press attention brought even more requests for backpacks.

Reporters sometimes get the name wrong. "They call it Sack It To *Me*, so I say I'm not sacking it to *myself*, I'm sacking it to *you*!"

A Cool Quarter-Million

To fill all the requests for supplies that poured in, Josh needed money. He mailed hundreds of letters asking for donations. Over five years, he has raised more than a

quarter of a million dol-
lars. But like many new
companies, Sack It To
You! is always strapped
for cash. Once, Josh
promised 76 backpacks to
a program called
Summerbridge to be
delivered in June. He
was expecting 2,500
packs from Office Depot in

late May but they were delayed. So he called a local company and begged for a donation for the backpacks. "It
always works out somehow," Josh says.

Collecting money is only the first step. Stuffing hundreds of backpacks would take one person hours and
hours. So Josh corrals his friends to pick up the supplies
and backpacks from local stores and his two storage centers, and help him to pack them.

When filling the backpacks, Josh follows Palm Beach
County's school supply list, with exceptions: "If an agency
wants tissues, I give them tissues." Elementary school kids
get things like pencils, crayons, and blunt-tipped scissors.
Middle and high school students' slightly bigger backpacks are filled with red marking pencils, pens, high-
lighters, sharp scissors, paper, notepads, and file folders.

Everybody also gets three big gluesticks. "The order
for gluesticks got messed up," says Josh. "I asked for 1,200
and they gave me 1,200 dozen." That's 14,400 gluesticks!

To stuff the backpacks, kids form an assembly line, one
person adding pens, another paper, and another scissors,
until each pack is full. "I try to make it fun," Josh says.

"We put on music and order pizza and work on the packs for a couple hours, then play basketball or something, then go back to work." All the packs are personalized, sporting a luggage tag with the Sack It To You! logo and the student's name. "I want kids to feel special—that their backpack is *theirs*," says Josh.

Sometimes the Marcus house resembles a warehouse. Piled in the den, living room, and hallway are white Office Depot bags stuffed with backpacks. "My brother moved out a couple years ago, so the bags have taken over his room," Josh says. Scrawled on each plastic bag in black marker is the name of the church or school where the supplies are headed.

When the backpacks are ready to go, Josh and his family and friends load the bags into his mom's truck to deliver them to the 17 agencies that request supplies.

Before handing out the packs to kids, Josh tells them: "If you want to do something, you do it. Don't let anyone stand in your way."

Supplies for All

Josh wants to give every student who needs supplies a full backpack. To do this, he wishes kids all over the country would start chapters of Sack It To You! Several kids have already agreed.

But Josh knows that Sack It To You! is an imperfect solution. "It's only one company and I'm only one person, and I realize that I can't help everybody." To explain why he keeps on going, he tells this story:

An old man strolled down the beach at dawn. He noticed a young man pick up a starfish and fling it into the sea. The old man asked: "Why are you doing this?" The young man answered that a stranded starfish would die if left in the morning sun.

"But the beach goes on for miles and there are millions of starfish," countered the old man. "How can you ever make a difference?"

The young man looked at a starfish in his hands, then threw it safely into the waves. "It makes a difference to this one," he said.

Still, the work can seem daunting. "Sometimes I just want to give it all up," he says. "It gets overwhelming because I want to do other things, like I really want to go play basketball, I really want to go outside or watch TV, but I know I have an obligation. It's an honor."

WHAT YOU CAN DO
Participate in a school fundraiser
Donate school supplies and books
Tutor a younger student

Put Your Pencils Down

Hannah Jukovsky

TEST BOYCOTTER

"The link between income and test scores should make people second-guess this whole one-shot-deal, quick band-aid fix for deeply rooted problems." **—Hannah Jukovsky**

One crisp November day, at a student rights forum at the Boston Public Library, middle and high school students began swapping stories about their schools.

"We don't have enough textbooks to go around," complained one boy from an inner-city school. "We have to share books, so you can't even take one home to do homework."

"That's weird," said a girl from a suburban school. "We have so many textbooks that sometimes teachers give us one to take home and another to leave at school!"

"How big are your classes?" one student asked while riffling through his backpack.

"Oh, I'd say about 20 students," said another kid.

"No way, it's more like 40 in our school," said another boy leaning forward with his elbows on his knees. "Sometimes we have to sprint to class just to get a seat!"

The discussion was an eye-opener for Hannah Jukovsky, a student at Cambridge Rindge and Latin, a public high school in Cambridge, Massachusetts. "Having all these different kids in the same room exposed disparities in education in such a concrete and immediate way," she says. "It really drove home the point that kids were getting a completely different deal on education in the state."

This Test Flunks!

The students had one thing in common: they all would have to pass a test—the Massachusetts Comprehensive Assessment System or MCAS—to get their diplomas.

The kids wondered: Was it really fair to deny diplomas to students from poor, overcrowded schools based on one test?

In fact, they decided, the test wasn't really fair to anybody. "You can get straight A's and fail MCAS and not graduate high school," Hannah says. "What if you had a bad day or you're just not good at taking tests?"

The test covered topics that many kids never studied in class. When Hannah took the eighth-grade MCAS, it had a question on Nubian sculpture. "Not about sculpture in general or trends in sculpture, but rather, how could I tell if this vase was Nubian?" There was a question on Chinese tomatoes. The fourth-grade test had a question about a frigate, a kind of boat. "I mean, you needed yachting experience to pass this test," Hannah says.

The kids worried that MCAS siphoned scarce funds from the classroom. Teachers, they believe, are terribly underpaid. "I was at a pizza parlor and—*ta-da!*—my eighth-grade science teacher was working there," says Hannah. "My homeroom teacher is a waitress at night. It's ridiculous." Some schools, instead of paying teachers more or buying new textbooks, spent money on test preparation packets, fearing that students would flunk.

The test also wasted valuable classroom time. At 17 hours, MCAS is longer than the New York State Bar Exam—the test people take to become lawyers. MCAS interrupts class for two whole weeks.

Finally, the kids thought about who passes standardized tests and who doesn't. "You may do well on the test if your parents have exposed you to the types of things that are on the test, if their income level and level of education are high enough so that you do well on standardized tests," Hannah says. "The link between income and test scores should make people second-guess this whole one-shot-deal, quick band-aid fix for deeply rooted problems."

Trashing the Test

Kids complained to the school board and state legislators, but didn't feel they were being taken seriously. So they decided to boycott the test.

Banned from using the P.A. system or posting fliers in school without special approval from the superintendent, students stuck to word of mouth. "Phone trees, in my opinion, are the best thing that ever happened," Hannah says.

With a phone tree you can spread news quickly; one

person calls three people, each of whom calls three more people, who call three more people, and so on. "Before you do anything, start a phone tree," Hannah suggests. "Don't wait. Just copy a list of the phone numbers of people involved because keeping in touch is so important."

Still, recruiting boycotters was a challenge. Many students worried about what punishment they would suffer for their defiance. Would they be suspended? Expelled? Months before the test, the school board voted that boycotters would not be punished. But many students and parents found that hard to believe. And the school board didn't publicize their decision because they didn't want to encourage boycotters, Hannah says.

And ultimately, kids didn't want to risk losing their diplomas. "You are a student hanging on by one academic thread, so to speak," Hannah explains. "You are struggling, trying to make it through, you're not at the greatest school, but you are doing your best. Are you going to boycott MCAS and lose your diploma? People who do that are incredibly brave. But you should be able to get your voice heard without making it a crisis. It's ridiculous that to get the legislature's attention, we have to refuse to take the test. We have to risk our diplomas just to get heard."

Hannah especially bristles when people say that some kids are only boycotting because they think they would fail. "Kids who are struggling academically have as much right to boycott as anyone else," Hannah says.

Joining a group of protestors in western Massachusetts, Hannah and her friends opened the eastern branch of the Student Coalition for Alternatives to MCAS, or SCAM. They threw rallies and continued to meet with legislators and school board members. Sometimes the meetings got heated. "We'd be talking to the Board of Education or legislators—people over 40 with pretty cushy jobs—and they'd get really defensive and not really listen and yell and stuff," Hannah says. "It was pretty funny to see grown men and women get all worked up against 16-year-olds. We'd think: 'We must be winning, because they are so upset.'"

Hannah has been wowed by the people students have won over—the teachers' union, the AFL-CIO. "They are such big organizations and this all started out so small," she says. "It's always surprising to have adults on your side, truthfully." When Green Party presidential candidate Ralph Nader appeared at a rally, Hannah thought, "Whoa, this is crazy! This is much, much bigger than we ever imagined!"

Though Hannah has been a key activist, she considers herself more of a creative person than an organizer. In fact, her favorite work for SCAM was making sculptures for the rallies. "I'd rather draw or do artwork of any kind than be in charge of this craziness," she says. Nevertheless, Hannah plans because she must. "I'm a big procrastinating mess," she says. "I'm very scatterbrained. I'm incredibly forgetful. I need to write things down and I never do."

Eighty Students Strong

Hannah and her friends managed to recruit eighty students from Cambridge Rindge and Latin School to boycott the test. While their classmates slumped over the bubble-filled sheets, pencils in hand, the boycotters could have played hooky. Instead, to prove that they were not boycotting out of laziness, they attended school every day.

For the whole two weeks of testing, the students studied education. Hannah and other kids organized a "teach-in" about testing and fairness, and about how the Department of Education and school committees in Massachusetts work. To prove to adults that there are better ways students can show what they know, boycotters ran a portfolio workshop. Students displayed their best essays, artwork, and other material. "It was a symbolic act of the other sides of us as students that can't be measured by standardized tests," Hannah says. "And to show generally the complexity of getting an education."

The boycotters were not punished for their defiance—this year. Next year the state will deny diplomas to those who fail or refuse to take the test. Students plan to lobby the legislature for lasting change. "Boycotts are only a tactic in the long-term battle for improving education," Hannah says.

WHAT YOU CAN DO
Ask questions about testing in your state
Join the Parent Student Teacher Association
Run for a seat on the school board

IDEAS THAT CAN CHANGE THE WORLD

"Every school should have an after-school tutoring program where you hire people to help kids with things they did not understand that day. If they learn it that day, they won't fall that far behind. You could hire retired teachers or just anyone who is smart and can explain stuff clearly without lots of big words."

—Elizabeth Jager, age 11

"Schools would be much better if students decided on the laws for schools."

—Lena Eckert-Erdheim, age 12

"Students should get two sets of books for each subject. One book will be kept in class and the other home. This would prevent kids from being reluctant to carry books home for homework or not bringing books to class."

—Lonnell Fuches, age 14

"I have a very good education with everything I need in my school in top condition. I think schools like mine should donate to other schools."

—John Weldon, age 14

"A major issue in schools is lack of parental involvement. It's nearly nonexistent by junior and senior high. One reason is that parents don't understand what the child is learning. An answer to this is to allow parents to take classes along with kids."

—Kristen Palmer, age 12

 *"If parents don't have time to be involved in school and help with homework—like if the parents are working too much—the student should have sessions with their teacher twice a week to work on stuff they are not getting. Or we could bring people from the community in to act as the 'school parent' for that child."*

—Nick Janecke, age 14

YOUR SOLUTION!

Chapter Two

GIVE PEACE A CHANCE

"If you are patient in one moment of anger, you will escape a hundred days of sorrow."
                                                    —Chinese Proverb

In the United States, every minute 14 people are victims of violent crime.

Every half hour, someone is murdered.

Every day, 1,000 women are sexually assaulted.

Every day, 17,000 people are threatened or beaten up.

Every day, 17 kids are thrown out of school for carrying a gun.

Every day, 10 kids are shot and killed.

Every day, 40 more kids are wounded by gunfire.

Every year, one in ten schools is the scene of a serious violent crime.

Every month, 7 percent of eighth graders stay home from school because they are afraid of being bullied by another child.

Imagine a world where none of this happened. What would it be like?

You could walk down any street, at any time of day, in complete safety. There would be no bullies, and people wouldn't have to be afraid to help a stranger out. People would live side by side in peace, and disagreements would be resolved by negotiating, not fighting.

Every day, thousands of kids imagine this world and work toward it—choosing peace over violence. Here are two inspiring stories.

Peace Across the Street

Gabriella Contreras

PEACEKEEPER

"We made them realize that we're here and that we want peace."
—Gabriella Contreras

Lunchtime at Gabriella Contreras's elementary school was sometimes really scary. Riots broke out just across the street at Tucson High School. Police would block off the street, stopping traffic, and lock down the school until the fighting was under control. One day, while 9-year-old Gabriella and her classmates ate their sandwiches, they witnessed something even more incredible across the street.

Dressed in black, holding body-sized bulletproof shields, a S.W.A.T. (Special Weapons and Tactics) team jumped out of a truck and formed a line, pressing in toward the fighting high school students. One officer shouted through a bullhorn, urging the students to stop. Some teenagers, trying to hide from the officers, scrambled over the fence and sprinted through the elementary school grounds.

Most elementary school kids ran inside in fear, but Gabriella and her friends remained glued to the gate, watching across the street. "I wish somebody would do something to stop this," one of Gabriella's friends said.

"Why don't *we* do something?" Gabriella replied. So they asked their third-grade teacher if she had any poster board. With crayons and markers, they colored large signs: "Stop the Violence!" and "Make Hugs Not Drugs!"

Gabriella and her friends marched with signs that day and the next. The fighting continued, at first. But the elementary school kids felt better because they had taken some action. Every day, for the rest of the year, the kids marched back and forth along the gate facing the high school, holding up their signs so the students could see.

Cars driving by honked their encouragement. The high school students peered across the street, watching the daily protests. And slowly, the rioting stopped.

"We shined a light on what they were doing," Gabriella says. "The high schoolers realized that there are these little kids, these little eyes watching. They see what you're doing, they hear a little bit of what you're saying, they see how you dress, how you act. We made them realize that we're here and that we want peace."

Inner Peace

The next year, even though the fighting quieted down,

Gabriella wanted to show everybody that violence is preventable. Kids just need other ways to express how they feel and to be heard. "You can have peace in your own mental environment," Gabriella says, "maybe not the environment around you, but peace inside you. One way to get that is volunteering and helping others, learning more about the community, learning more about yourself."

So she invited her classmates to meet every Monday at lunchtime to talk about how they could prevent violence and strengthen their community. The first meeting was in the principal's office. But it was too small for the 50 kids who showed up. So they moved to the library. But they couldn't work in total silence. So they asked the fourth-grade teacher if they could use his room.

Gabriella dubbed the group Club BADDD. She had heard of SADD—Students Against Drunk Drivers—and MADD—Mothers Against Drunk Drivers. So she settled on BADDD, for Be Alert Don't Do Drugs. "I thought it was so awesome," says Gabriella. "Even now, students will go around saying: 'Yeah, I'm a BADDD student!'"

Kids wanted Club BADDD to be totally kid run, so they decided that everyone would sign in. The first kid to sign

in would open the meeting, the next would read the agenda, and the third would close the meeting.

In Club BADDD, troublemakers became leaders. "Students in the classroom who can't sit still or always have to talk first or talk with other students are usually labeled troublemakers," says Gabriella. "They join the club and at first they think they are going to be treated in the same way, where they can't talk, can't share their ideas." If they arrive early, they can open the meeting, read the agenda, or close the meeting. "All of a sudden they are in charge and students are listening to them," Gabriella says. "They are learning to use their leadership skills in a positive way."

Club BADD meetings always start with their motto: "Even as youth we can make a difference in our home, neighborhood, school, and community."

"I thought about water dropping in a lake and how it makes a ripple," Gabriella says. "How you can start at home and make a difference there and then you can make a difference in your school and you'll end up making a difference in your community."

Marching for Peace

The first ripple they attempted was an annual peace march around the elementary school to kick off the school year.

"You'll never get the whole school," adults told them. "You'll never make it happen every year." That made Gabriella steaming mad. "We *can* do this!" she protested.

Her mom told her not to argue with adults, just to show them that kids can make it happen.

But Club BADDD members got discouraged, too. Gabriella told them, "We have to go through with it and show them that we can."

So the kids met with the principal and convinced him that it was the right way to start the school year. With the principal on their side, the whole school marched. "It's not an everyday occurrence to see fifth graders and kinder-garteners and eighth graders and teachers and police and community members marching around a school," Gabriella says. "People didn't believe that such young students could do something so powerful and make that much of an impact."

Every year Club BADDD runs an anti-drug art gallery. Kids draw pictures about how they would say no to drugs or how they would stop violence. One child drew a girl in pigtails being offered drugs, shaking her finger toward them. On the other half of the page, the girl jumped rope with her friends. Underneath, the child wrote: "I'd rather be jumping rope than doing drugs!"

Club members painted over graffiti in the neighbor-hood. They raised money from bake sales to buy a bike for a student with cerebral palsy and to help a girl get a heart transplant. They cleaned up school grounds and repainted benches and trash cans. They wrote Valentine's Day and Thanksgiving cards for elderly people and delivered them in person. "We built bridges instead of doing what we see in the news all the time—kids tearing bridges down," she says. "Kids learned that they can do simple things and have a big impact."

Kid Power

Scholastic magazine ran a short article on Club BADDD. "All of a sudden, out of nowhere, I got bundles of mail asking about Club BADDD," Gabriella says. Kids from

New York, Alaska, California, and Florida wanted to know how to start a club in their school.

Gabriella didn't know how to respond. "I needed money to make a packet with brochures and a video to show kids how to do it, so it would be easy for them." Then one day at the library, she saw a flier with the word MONEY in big letters. A group called Pro-Neighborhood offered grants—money to support special projects—to community members. She called them and they invited her to a meeting to learn how to apply for a grant.

The room was full of adults. Gabriella, now 11 years old, was the only kid to show up. At one point, the speaker asked how much money people wanted. "I said I wanted the full amount, $2,500," Gabriella says. "I remember a lady laughing, saying: 'Goodness! A *child* is asking for that much money?! She wouldn't even know what to do with all that!'"

Gabriella told her: "Yes, I *would* know, because I already have an idea of what the packet would look like and how to do the video." All the adults became quiet and just stared at her.

"My mom would have stood up for me but she was out of town," says Gabriella. "And my dad figured it was a kid-oriented thing, so he just dropped me off and picked me up an hour later." Gabriella didn't let the adults get to her. She filled out the grant application and won the full $2,500.

Club members prepared a packet of information on how to start a club, how to run a meeting, how to handle money. The school video club helped them make a film showing a Club BADDD meeting, some of the events, and Gabriella talking about the club.

The kids were excited for the first viewing of the video. What a disappointment. The picture was shaky, the color was off, and the sound was muffled. "We got so quiet," Gabriella says. "We were happy we'd made a video, but we knew we should do it again." And they did.

The video wasn't the toughest challenge Club BADDD faced. Over the years, kids couldn't understand why anyone would join a club instead of playing during lunch. "Why don't you just try it," club members said. Once kids joined, they stayed. In fact over the years, more than 200 kids have been involved in Club BADDD.

"On TV, you don't see younger students making an impact," says Gabriella. "You see adults volunteering or you see violence and drugs and negativity, so kids don't think they can make a difference. Then, once they are in it, they realize that it's not just a facade that all these members are putting on—it's the truth. They really *are* making a difference. It empowers them."

WHAT YOU CAN DO

Organize a peace march at your school

Search for inner peace

Talk with friends about how to promote peace

Strong Stuff

Kirsten Wright

SELF-DEFENSE ADVOCATE

"Don't be afraid to voice your ideas. Don't be intimidated, because there are many people who feel the same way as you do."
—Kirsten Wright

At thirteen, Kirsten Wright of Twin Falls, Idaho, started to worry about other girls her age. She read newspaper and magazine articles about girls who wandered into dangerous situations and couldn't get out. "I remember reading about a girl who had one drink at a party and woke up the next morning to find she'd been drugged and attacked during the night," says Kirsten.

Kirsten wanted girls to be able to stand up for themselves. Since the third grade, she had been learning self-defense techniques in martial arts classes. "I wanted other girls to learn what they could do to avoid dangerous situations and protect themselves," she says. Kirsten's martial arts teacher sometimes held special self-defense classes for women. "But this stuff isn't just for grown women," Kirsten says. "It should be for girls who are just beginning to be independent and date and get in relationships."

Taking Charge

So Kirsten decided to hold a two-day seminar on self-defense for girls. When Kirsten first told her friends about her idea, some said, "Are you crazy? Do you really want to put that together?"

"I'm normally the kind of person who just sits back and does what people tell me to do," says Kirsten. "I really didn't believe that I was the kind of person to take charge until I became really concerned about other girls and I felt that the class needed to happen."

She wanted girls to have a safe, unthreatening place to learn self-defense skills. "I remember my first martial-arts class—I was frightened because I was small and other people there were bigger and had a lot of self-confidence," she says.

Her martial arts teacher offered his studio and his time for the classes, but Kirsten wanted other speakers, too. She wanted someone to talk with girls about how to stay safe while on a date. She also wanted to warn them about date-rape drugs. "Someone can slip something in your food or drink causing you to become disoriented or sleepy," she explains.

Rape and assault are really unpleasant topics for a young teenage girl to think about. And inviting strangers to speak at the seminar was not easy. "I'm kind of shy,"

Kirsten says, "so the hardest thing for me was getting enough confidence to talk openly with people about this subject."

Slowly easing into the topic helped. "When I spoke with the school counselor, I just started a normal conversation and then brought up what I wanted to do."

Kirsten really admires police officers, but she was intimidated inviting one to speak at the seminar. "They are these big guys in the black outfits and they don't grin that much," she says. "But once I got into the subject of wanting to help others, they were very warm and nice."

Kirsten thinks it's important to overcome your fears and do what you believe. "Don't be afraid to voice your ideas," she says. "Don't be intimidated, because there are many people who feel the same way as you do."

Since Kirsten is a Girl Scout, to recruit girls, she sent fliers to all the scout leaders in the area. She asked them to pass registration forms on to their girls to sign up.

The Big Day

The first day of the class, Kirsten's martial arts teacher, the police officer, the school counselor, and tons of girls gathered in Jerome Martial Arts Academy—with its mirrored walls, smooth floors, and punching bags and pads.

After an introduction from the police officer, the martial arts instructor gave tips on how to prevent violence. Be aware of your surroundings, and if someone approaches you, watch his body language, he said.

Keep your head up high and stand up straight, he continued, demonstrating a proud and straight posture. If you hunch or look at the ground, you might appear weaker, less confident, and more vulnerable to an attacker.

If someone does grab you, try passive resistance first, the instructor said. The girls were surprised at one of his suggestions: Vomit on the attacker and he may get disgusted and move away.

Then he showed the girls how to escape. If you are ever attacked, don't yell *Help!* Some people will ignore that because they don't want to get involved, the martial arts instructor told them. Yell *Fire!* so people will think their lives could be in danger, and they'll come over and see what is going on and get involved, and try to help you.

Then the instructor and the girls brainstormed everyday items they could use to fight back: car keys, a comb, and a pencil.

The Right Moves

On the second day, the school counselor talked with the girls about how to stay safe on a date. Be assertive, she said. Never be pressured to do something you don't want to do. Also, be careful about what you eat and drink at parties. She handed out fliers with information about how to get help if anything ever happened.

This was pretty heavy stuff, and Kirsten wanted the girls to have fun, too. "When you don't have fun, you start to not pay attention," she says. So she asked her martial arts instructor to show the girls some basic self-defense moves.

The girls practiced the techniques with their friends. They learned the "grab counter." If someone grabs your wrist, you rotate your wrist and get your hand on top to hold their hand while you use your other arm to deflect the other arm. "The girls would get in odd positions with one girl on top of another pinning her down," says Kirsten. "The girl on the bottom would start to giggle and they'd both really laugh a lot." But they all learned how to do the moves.

At the end of the class, Kirsten asked the girls to fill out evaluations so she could make the seminar even better the next time. Most of the girls wrote, "It was really fun!" and "Good job!" and "I hope you do it again so my little sister can learn this."

That convinced Kirsten to organize another class, with a few changes: the next one will be open to the whole community, as well as the Girl Scouts. And Kirsten is going to get the local hospital involved. "When I move on and can't do this anymore, I want them to keep it going for all teens who need these skills," she says.

WHAT YOU CAN DO
Organize a school crime patrol
Learn self-defense
Join a neighborhood watch

IDEAS THAT CAN CHANGE THE WORLD

"We could try not to take sides. Taking sides results in war. All the world governments should develop a policy of not taking sides. This needs to be worldwide to stop war."

—Ethan Temple, age 10

"Today, violent people are fined, put in jail, or even put to death. But there are still many crimes being committed. My idea is to reward peaceful or lawful people with awards or money instead of forcing them to be good or face the consequences. Most would rather do as they were told if rewarded for doing right than be punished for doing wrong. To enforce laws, people above the age of 30 with no criminal record could be rewarded with money or some other kind of gift. Even children in school could be rewarded for peaceful behavior."

—Hannah Hironaka, age 12

"Half of violence is revenge. If someone punches you, you want to punch back. To stop violence is to never start it, so we should teach people a better way to solve problems. When I was lit-

tle, I was taught to talk, walk, and squawk. Talk to the other person, tell them to stop. Walk away from a conflict. Squawk to someone who can help. Those are good rules to live by." **—Graham Klag, age 14**

"If we stop selling guns, there would not be as much of violence. For all the people that already have guns, we should have a voucher. We could give each person a hundred dollars to one hundred and fifty when they turn in their guns. Then I bet mostly everyone will do it." **—Jade Harvey, age 13**

"We need to be very kind to people and tell them they are doing good. It's like the old story about a village where people kept telling a young boy that he's a bad boy. They named him Bad Young Boy and then all he did was bad things. When people started calling him Good Young Boy, all he did was good things."

—Catherine Schrage, age 10

YOUR SOLUTION!

Chapter Three

THE WORLD'S TABLE

"Enough is equal to a feast."—Henry Fielding

The lunch bell rings. You jump from your desk, ready to race to the cafeteria.

"Not so fast," says your teacher. "Today we're serving a special lunch, called World Lunch."

"I'm starving," you mutter to your friend as you wait in line with your 30 classmates for your meal ticket. Yours is red. Your friend's is green.

"Green tickets first," the teacher says. Your friend and three other kids are escorted to a large table with four chairs. Covering the table is a white tablecloth. Elegant silverware, plates, and glasses stand in front of each chair.

The teacher carries pizza slices, hamburgers, turkey and cheese sandwiches, apples, carrots, cookies, milk, juice, and soda to that table.

Look at all that food! Those four kids will never be able to eat it all.

Rice and Beans

"People with yellow tickets sit at this table," the teacher says, pointing to a long table with paper plates holding small mounds of rice and beans. Eighteen kids sit down, grumbling.

"Rice and beans are boring," one says.

"Hey, you got more rice than me," another complains.

"I have soccer practice after school," a girl argues. "I need more lunch." When the teacher doesn't respond to their protests, the kids begin to eat.

You and seven other students shuffle your feet, waiting.

"Red ticket holders," the teacher says. "Please sit in a circle on the floor." Your stomach growls as you wonder what is in store for you.

Your teacher leaves the room and returns with a pitcher of muddy-looking water and one pot of rice. She places the food and water in the center of the circle, hands each student a spoon and a small cup and says, "Help yourself."

You watch in astonishment as the other kids shovel the lumpy rice into their mouths as fast they can. "Gross," you think. But then you notice the rice is disappearing fast. You scoop a few bites into your cup before it's all gone. The rice sticks to the roof of your mouth. You raise your hand. "Can we drink this water?" you ask. "It looks dirty."

Hunger and Thirst

The teacher explains that you can drink the water—it's clean water tinted with food coloring. But the *one-and-a-half billion* people worldwide that you and the seven other red ticket holders represent are not so lucky. Those people—25 percent of the world's population—do not have access to clean water. Living in countries such as Ethiopia, Haiti, and Cambodia, these people never get enough food to eat. Each year, twenty million die of starvation or hunger-related illnesses.

Barely Enough

The rice-and-beans kids—60 percent of your class, and 60 percent of the world—get just enough to eat. Families in this group—living in Eastern Europe, Thailand, and the United States—eat three meals a day most of the time. But sometimes they have to skip meals or eat less than they need because money is tight. In a recent survey, a quarter of Americans said that at some point in the past year, someone in their family had too little money to buy enough food. Almost half of the people who get groceries from food banks are from working families.

You look hungrily at the feast of bread, meat, fruits, vegetables, and milk in front of four of your classmates. They represent the 15 percent of people who have more than enough to eat. Most live in the United States, Australia, France, and other Western European countries.

The four students squirm in their chairs, uncomfortable. They are full, but piles of food remain. About 250,000 people could be fed for a whole year with the food that Americans waste in one day.

Some people think that we can never solve world hunger because there is not enough food to go around. But right now, the world has enough food for every person to get four and a half pounds of food each day: two and half pounds of grains, beans, and nuts; about a pound of fruits and vegetables; and almost a pound of meat, milk, and eggs. The problem is that many people cannot afford the food they so desperately need.

All this is enough to make you feel guilty each time you sit down to a meal. But you can get past the guilt and take action—check out what these kids did.

Breakfast Bonanza!

Zachary Ebers

CEREAL-DRIVE COORDINATOR

"You don't need to be really, really intelligent to make a big difference. All you need is the desire to help somebody." —Zachary Ebers

Zachary Ebers, of St. Louis, Missouri, starts his day each morning with a bowl of Fruit Loops or Cinnamon Toast Crunch cereal. An avid player of sports—baseball, basketball, volleyball, hockey, and soccer—Zach says breakfast gives him the energy he needs to make it through a game.

That's why when he toured Feed My People, a food pantry for needy families near his home, he noticed that they had only five boxes of cereal. Stacked on the shelves were canned corn, peas, green beans, and Spaghettio's, but not much for breakfast. During the school year, poor kids get free breakfast at school. But Zach wondered:

What do they eat in the morning during the summer?

Zach's family isn't rich, but he eats three meals a day. "Hunger would be so horrible," Zach says. "Going to bed not knowing what you are going to eat the next morning, or if you were going to get anything to eat at all."

Zach considered volunteering at a food pantry. "But I thought if I took action into my own hands, if I designed a whole other program, I could get more people involved," he says.

So he asked all his friends on his sports teams and some of his cousins if they would collect cereal at their schools or churches. "I wanted a catchy name for what we were doing and I knew breakfast was part of it," he says. "We wanted something that would almost rhyme or begin with the same letter." He looked in the dictionary under B and found "bonanza," which means, a source of great wealth. "So if we collected a wealth of cereal, it would be a Breakfast Bonanza!"

Each school or church has a Breakfast Bonanza coordinator—usually a kid—who spreads the word, collects the cereal, and picks a needy pantry. Zach drafted letters for the coordinators to show to their principals or church leaders, explaining the need for cereal and how a cereal-drive works. He made fliers for his friends to copy and hand out to publicize the drives. Zach wanted food pantries to be stocked with cereal in the summer months, so he decided to run the drives in the spring. In May and June, the drives began.

Cereal Roundup

A typical cereal drive lasts about a week. Most school cereal drives start on a Monday. The kids had no idea how many boxes would trickle in. So they were shocked when by Friday a huge pile of cereal boxes, more than a hundred, would stand along the wall of a hallway or storage room. " A hundred boxes of cereal, oh my gosh, that is tons of cereal," Zach says.

In the first year of Breakfast Bonanza, Zach and his friends ran seven drives, collecting 800 boxes of cereal for the summer. "I was just doing what I could to help," he says. "I didn't know how successful we would be. It was kind of amazing."

Kid coordinators count the boxes and arrange for cars to deliver them to food pantries around the city. Once piled on food pantry shelves, the cereal boxes cover a whole wall. There they stay until summer starts. Because poor kids really need breakfast in the summer, Zach asked food pantries to wait till school ended to distribute the cereal. He also requested the cereal go to families with children and that each child be allowed pick out their own box.

"When kids come 'shop' for their box, you should see the smiles!" Zach says.

Sometimes it's hard to know how much your work helps. Once, while Zach unloaded cereal boxes for Feed My People, a volunteer there told him that some kids had been in the day before and were disappointed that all the cereal was gone. "They'll be so happy when I tell them we have cereal again," she told him.

For the next year, Zachary set a goal of collecting 2,000 boxes. He recruited 18 groups—from St. Francis of Assisi to Southside Christian Church to Rogers Elementary—to participate. A Wal-Mart was opening nearby, so Zachary convinced them to donate 600 boxes, for a grand total of 2,541 boxes.

On Top of Things

Organizing something like this means talking to lots of people. "I'm not too good at speaking out and talking to principals," Zach says. "Before I went to a school, I thought about what I would say. I wrote it out and said it to myself because I was so nervous."

To keep everything straight, Zach wrote down all the organizations and their contact information. If any information was missing—like when the drive happened, how many boxes they collected, or what pantry they delivered to—he called them back.

Keeping tabs was tough. "I had to call people and schools and everybody was so busy," Zach says. "I had to make tons of phone calls. They'd say they'd get back to me but sometimes they didn't call back. Then I had to get ahold of them."

When Zach called around to the kid coordinators the third year, he discovered that some had dropped the ball. Breakfast Bonanza usually collects cereal in May or June for the summer, and by the time he called, it was too late to get the drives going. Totals were down slightly, to around 1,600 boxes. But that didn't worry Zach. In fact, it just made him work harder. "I'm going to stay on top of it and really build it up," he says.

Dedication can make it happen. Zach considers himself to be an average kid. "You don't need to be really, really intelligent to make a big difference," he says. "All you need is the desire to help somebody."

WHAT YOU CAN DO

Find out what local food banks need

Organize or participate in a food drive

Sort, package, and hand out food at a food bank

Eat Your Vegetables

Dusty Hill

ORGANIC GARDENER

"I didn't like that we would bring food one week, then not again for another three weeks." **—Dusty Hill**

When he was diagnosed with cancer, Dustin Hill of Portland, Oregon, wondered what would happen to the vegetable garden he had planted to fight hunger. It was June, Dusty had just finished sixth grade, and the garden—and the weeds—had just begun to really grow.

Dusty got the idea for the garden while preparing packages of oranges, cookies, mittens, and socks with his family, to hand out to needy people at Christmastime. Orange in hand, Dusty thought about how food drives at schools collect lots of canned goods. "But food banks and soup kitchens don't really get fresh produce very often," Dusty says.

So in January, Dusty invited 12 friends from his neighborhood and his school to help him grow vegetables for hungry people. "It's so much easier with a bunch of kids than doing it alone," says Dusty.

The group dubbed themselves PlanIt Kids. To get the garden started, they got a $490 grant from Take the Time, a community program to empower young people. "It wasn't that hard to apply," Dusty says. "On the application we had to tell them about our project, what we were going to do, the cost of materials, pretty simple questions." A month later they got the money. "I was excited because I knew it was really going to happen," Dusty says.

Learn As You Go

The kids didn't always know what they were doing. "None of us had ever gardened before," says Dusty. "We just kind of went at it. We didn't know when to water or how to plant seeds." So the kids read the backs of the seed packets, watched gardening shows on TV, and asked their parents for tips.

In April, they pressed seeds into the soil of dozens of tiny plastic boxes. They kept the sprouts inside by a sunny window for the first few weeks.

After waiting for five dry days in a row—a rare event in the rainy Pacific Northwest—the kids tilled the ground. They cut and placed lumber in large rectangles to hold the soil in raised beds. To battle the mud, they poured bark dust on the pathways.

PlanIt Kids planted cucumbers, tomatoes, zucchini, beans, peas, and peppers. They planted tiny pumpkins, and herbs: parsley, sage, and rosemary.

The kids wanted people to have the freshest, healthiest vegetables possible. So instead of spraying weed-killers, the kids decided to get the weeds the old fashioned way— by pulling them.

Two Battles

The battle between the vegetables and the weeds had just begun when Dustin discovered a lump above his knee. "When we were driving home after baseball or soccer games, my dad would always pat me on my leg and it really hurt," he says. The doctors diagnosed a rare soft-tissue tumor, and said they wanted to remove it as soon as possible.

"It was a big setback," Dusty says. "When I left for the hospital for surgery, I wondered if the garden would make it."

The garden is in Dusty's backyard, a slice of country just minutes from downtown Portland, down a gravel road deeply rutted with potholes. The light-blue farmhouse sits back from the road, with rakes, hoes, and a shovel hanging from pegs on the side of the garage.

Out back, past the patio with its wicker porch swing and potted flowers, a beat-up picnic table rests beneath a crab-apple tree. There, just beyond the table, is the organic garden tended by PlanIt Kids. Bunches of orange and yellow marigolds mark the corners of nine raised beds and keep the bugs out. Beans crawl up a tepee trellis. The whole place smells of damp earth and freshly cut wood.

When Dusty left for the hospital that first spring, the garden had just been planted and weeded. Dusty worried that while he was fighting the cancer, the weeds would strangle the vegetable plants and destroy the garden.

Dusty returned home from the hospital a few weeks later to some good news. "While I was gone, all the kids pitched in and weeded," says Dusty. "When I came home, the plants were so huge. They even put a lounge chair out so I could just sit out there. It was cool."

While he recovered, Dusty watched and weeded as much as he could. "I tried to bend down, but that didn't really work out that well," he says.

Some vegetables were ready for picking in July. Dusty couldn't reach down to pluck them, so the other PlanIt Kids filled two big baskets with dozens of cucumbers and huge zucchini. By August, though he was still on crutches and going to physical therapy, Dusty's leg felt better. Dusty celebrated with a harvest. "We filled tons of baskets with tomatoes!" Dusty said.

Hospitality and Hope

PlanIt Kids had to decide where to donate the veggies. Dusty's mom suggested Sisters of the Road Cafe. Sisters of the Road serves up more than soup. It serves up hospitality and hope. "I like their philosophy," Dusty says, "of nonviolence and dignity."

Not your typical soup kitchen, Sisters of the Road looks more like a diner. You chose from two meals and some sides. After ordering at the counter, you snag a stool at the counter or sit at one of the tables. While you wait, you can watch food preparations in the opening to the kitchen.

"It smells like a really good restaurant," Dusty says. "Like when you're near the kitchen and the whole place smells like food. The rice and beans look really yummy, too."

In fact, Sisters of the Road doesn't like to be called a soup kitchen. They prefer the dignity of the label "nonprofit cafe." Meals cost $1.25 per person. But no one goes hungry. People who have no money can pay for their meals by wiping down tables, sweeping the floor, or slicing vegetables.

Sisters of the Road makes good use of the produce PlanIt Kids donates. They dice the tomatoes into fresh salsa. They make zucchini into fresh bread and tasty bean dishes—even zucchini pie.

New Life, New Ideas

A year after starting the garden, Dusty's doctors said the tumor was gone. With his whole life ahead of him, Dusty felt good about the garden, but something bothered him. "I didn't like that we would bring food one week, then not again for another three weeks." So Dusty went back to Take the Time to ask for more money—this time to pay for fruit the kids would harvest from U-Pick farms. With 50 dollars each week, the kids could pick and buy 100 pounds of berries—berries that another Sisters project, Boxcar Bertha's, could blend into fruit smoothies, tuck into fruit pancakes, bake into fresh fruit pies. They also pick corn, beans, and tomatoes as they come into season.

Every Friday in the summer, the kids go berry picking, filling large flats and big bags full of marionberries, blackberries, loganberries, raspberries, boysenberries, peaches, strawberries, and blueberries. It's hot and sweaty work, but fun. Kids compete to harvest the most berries, and they sneak samples of the tempting fruit as they pick.

Once one of the kids ate so many berries that his teeth were stained purple. "He was really worried that he would get in trouble from the people at the cash register, so he talked with his mouth closed!" Dusty recalls.

Give a Little, Get a Lot

Picking fruit at different farms got PlanIt Kids thinking. If every farm gave just a little, Sisters of the Road would have enough for a big feast. It's like that old tale, "Stone Soup," Dusty says, where a visitor creates a delicious soup from water and a stone by tricking villagers into donating carrots, potatoes, meat, and spices to add to the pot.

When PlanIt Kids learned that Sisters of the Road throws a big free feast twice a year, they wanted to give the stone-soup approach a try. They offered to host a feast, so Sisters added a third. You won't believe some of the items on the grocery list for this barbecue: 350 pounds of chicken, 400 ears of corn, 200 pounds of potatoes, 100 pounds of flour, 25 pounds of sugar, and 3 gallons of mayonnaise and mustard. And that's just half of it.

"We just called little places," Dusty says. "Little farms and little markets. We called an onion farm and got 50 pounds of onions. We found that little places are much easier to deal with than the big corporations, who would say, 'Oh we'll get back to you in a year to see if your donation request was approved.'"

Under the guidance of Sisters' cooks, PlanIt Kids helped serve barbecued chicken, fresh corn, potato salad, corn bread, and lemonade—for more than 400 people!

Feeding people feels so good, and growing a garden is so much fun, that Dusty wants other kids to try it. "Now I want to spread the word about hunger and do gardens all across Portland and get kids started in other places," he says. He's going to make a packet of material to send to kids who want to start a garden to fight hunger. He'll include tips, seeds, and encouraging words.

"I still worry about how many hungry people there are," Dusty says. "But I feel I'm doing the best I can, and it's helping the people I can help."

WHAT YOU CAN DO
Plant a garden and donate the harvest
Volunteer at a soup kitchen
Ask local farms to donate

Stone Soup

A woman trudges into a remote town, hungry. She knocks on doors asking for food, but the villagers stash their food away and say: "Sorry, we don't have any."

So the woman stands in the town square and declares: "I am a master chef and if someone brings me a large pot, I'll make some magical stone soup!" A curious villager peeks her head out of the door and says: "I have a big soup pot."

"If only I had an onion..." the visitor says.

"I have an onion," one villager exclaims, running back to his house.

"Great!" she says. "It would be even better with a carrot."

"I'll go get one," another villager says.

"Hmm, I wish we had a potato..." the old woman mutters.

This goes on until the pot is brimming with fresh vegetables, meats, and spices—enough to feed the whole town!

After the villagers eat their fill, one asks: "What is the magical ingredient in your wonderful soup?"

"Sharing," the woman answers.

IDEAS THAT CAN CHANGE THE WORLD

"Families with enough food should go out and find three poor people who usually don't have enough food, and invite them to their house for the night and share dinner with them. Then they'd find three more people for the next night. So you'd have three different people in your house every night, and that should take a bite out of world hunger." **—Daniel Lakin, age 13**

"We could have a certain type of foam that would have all the protein and minerals a plant would need to grow. We would give this—and some plant seeds—to the hungry for free. It would be easy for them to plant because it would be indoors instead of outdoors in soil." **—Tamara Furshpan, age 15**

"Give the starving people a loan with no interest and help them get back on their feet, then once they're more prosperous they can pay back the loan. If they never pay you back, it would be okay; it would be money well spent."

—Juzar Jamnagerwalla, age 15

"Restaurants should be required to make at least ten meals for the poor a day. Not any extraordinary meals where the restaurant would lose money, just simple meals. Maybe a bowl of soup, a small salad, maybe a chicken cutlet."

—Kaitlyn Lauletta, age 13

"My solution is for the government to supply funds for farmers to buy more land to grow more crops. The more crops we have of fruits and vegetables, the more food we would have for the hungry."

—Marguerite Hyun-Ok Roberge, age 12

YOUR SOLUTION!

Chapter Four

YOUR PLANET

"Whatever we do affects everything and everyone else, if even in the tiniest way. Why, when a housefly flaps his wings, a breeze goes round the world; when a speck of dust falls to the ground, the entire planet weighs a little more; and when you stomp your foot, the earth moves slightly off its course."
—Norton Juster, *The Phantom Tollbooth*

Would you throw away a $20 bill? Of course not! What if the bill had been used a lot already, if it was worn out and dirty? Would you toss it in the trash? No way! You know that even if a $20 bill has been used, it's still worth the same amount.

That's true of a lot of stuff we toss into the trash. Take a soda can, for example. Lots of work has already gone into making that can. Metal was dug out of the earth and impurities were removed. That work is wasted if you throw out that can. It takes 20 times more energy to make a soda can from scratch than from a recycled can.

Since it takes less energy to make products from garbage than from scratch, recycling causes less pollution. Forming a new soda can from an old one creates 95 percent less air pollution than making a can from scratch. Creating new paper from 2,000 pounds of old paper keeps 7,000 gallons of water from being treated with chemicals—and saves 17 trees. Making a new juice bottle from an old one cuts air pollution by about 20 percent.

You might not think that every can or notepaper or bottle you throw away is worth very much—but if you add it all up, our garbage dumps are really gold mines!

Every year, Americans throw out enough aluminum to remake all the airplanes in the country four times over. We throw away enough white paper to build a 12-foot high wall from coast to coast. We throw out enough glass to fill 52 skyscrapers from the basement to the top floor.

But the real reason to recycle has nothing to do with money. We share our planet with other creatures that don't have the ability to protect—or destroy—the earth the way we do. Take the smallest thing, like brushing your teeth. Turning off the water when you brush saves more than a thousand gallons of water a year.

In this chapter, you'll read about kids who know that our actions affect this planet. And they are already working on new solutions and inventions for protecting the planet and keeping it healthy for years to come.

Don't Be Crude

Lacy Jones, Kate Klinkerman, and Barbara Brown

CLEAN-WATER WATCHDOGS

"In different places there are different environmental issues. Look around your community and see what needs to be done there." —Kate Klinkerman

When Kate Klinkerman was 11, she saw her dad dump motor oil from the family's truck onto some weeds alongside their barn. A few days later, Kate noticed something. All the weeds had died, leaving nothing but bare blackened earth. Kate asked her dad about it. "He poured the oil on the weeds on purpose," Kate says. "It's kind of hard to get at them with the lawnmower."

Kate wondered: If the oil seeps far enough into the ground to kill the weeds, could it do more damage? "We get our drinking water from a well on our land," Kate says.

"So clean groundwater is really important." To Kate's horror, she learned that the amount of oil in one oil change can ruin a day's supply of water for a small city.

Kate called her friends Barbara Brown and Lacy Jones. Does your dad change the oil in your cars himself? "Yes," they said. Have you ever seen him pour it on the ground? "Yes," they replied.

The girls live in Victoria County, Texas, a rural area two hours south of Houston. "It's called the crossroads because we lie between Houston, San Antonio, and Corpus Christi," says Kate.

The land where they live is flat and fertile, mostly fields of cotton, soybeans, and corn. Farmers there pride themselves on keeping up their tractors and trucks—and that includes changing the oil themselves.

"If you live in town and you get your oil changed at the local service station, the oil is automatically recycled," Kate says. "That's the law in Texas. But some people, like farmers, just dump it on the ground. They've been doing it for years and years, not knowing any better, not knowing it contaminated the groundwater."

The Girls Take Over

Barbara knew someone from her church who worked at an oil recycling company, Spill Response, Inc. The girls paid them a visit. Located in town, Spill Response is a small outfit: a building, some tanks, and a couple trucks. The manager gladly showed them around and explained how tanker trucks pick up used oil and pump it into the recycling center. They screen the oil to catch leaves and trash, then separate water from the oil. The water is cleaned and put back into local rivers and the used oil is taken to another company that recycles it into material to build roads.

Spill Response told the girls that the Texas Natural Resource Conservation Commission had tried to start a grant program to promote oil recycling in rural areas. They even had T-shirts and bumper stickers with a catchy name: Don't Be Crude. But few towns wanted to participate, so they canceled the program.

"It was kind of luck that we came across Don't Be Crude," says Kate. The girls had been looking for a good 4-H project, something they could do to take care of the environment and help their community. They knew Don't Be Crude was it.

"The resources we have now, like our water supply and our oil supply, aren't going to last forever," Kate says. "We need to think about how we can conserve them for our kids and for our kids' kids."

The girls asked the conservation commission and the Victoria County Commissioner if they could take on Don't Be Crude. At first, many people thought: "Sixth graders? What can sixth graders do?" says Kate. "But it doesn't matter how young you are."

The TNRCC donated boxes of Don't Be Crude materials and granted approval for five oil recycling sites:

Windmill Country Store, the Raisin Windmill Country Store, William Wood Elementary, and two county road maintenance centers. "We'd like to put one near a feed store, because they get lots of traffic from farmers," says Kate.

At first the girls placed black metal 55-gallon barrels at the sites. "But those were really hard to see," Kate says. "And when people tried to dump their oil into the small hole, it ended up spilling on the ground causing an even bigger problem than the one we wanted to stop in the first place." With so much oil seeping into one spot, the girls knew the soil wouldn't keep the oil from reaching the groundwater.

The girls went to the Web. They found a company in Florida that sells 460-gallon puncture-proof recycling containers, with a large opening for pouring in the oil, a strainer that catches any trash in the oil, and a small gauge that says when it's full.

The downside: they cost $2,000 each. So the girls wrote letters to local businesses, such as Dupont and Dow Chemicals, requesting donations. They raised $6,000, enough for three containers.

The girls eventually won nonprofit status for their project and approval for a total of eight sites in two counties. U.S. Filters offered to pick up and recycle the oil—and oil filters—for free.

On the Road

Placing containers around the region was not enough. "A big part of the project is telling the public about where the recycling centers are and that they *need* to recycle," says Kate. So the girls have taken their show on the road, visiting schools and other 4-H clubs with their message.

"We had no idea how much oil would be recycled," Kate says. "It started off little, so we didn't imagine that we would collect over 30,000 gallons." Now people stop her and the other girls and say proudly: I have recycled my oil!

Don't Be Crude has expanded to Calhoun County, a coastal area where dumped oil can leech into a bay. A 4-H club in Calhoun volunteered to run the recycling program there. "If it works there, we're going to train other 4-H'ers to start their own projects and let them run them," Kate says. "We'd like it to spread across Texas."

Kate teases her dad about being the bad guy who got the whole thing started, calling him the "Crude" in Don't Be Crude. "He's really good about it, he just laughs it off," Kate says. "Most people who live out here can relate, because they've done it, too."

And there's a lesson in that. "We always want to blame big business for our problems," says Kate. "But you need to look at home. Many times you are the one that's pollut-

ing, and you need to look at what you can do to help the environment."

"Look at where you live," Kate says. "In the community I live in, dumping oil alongside the barn is a big issue. But in different places, there are different environmental issues. Look around your community and see what needs to be done there."

WHAT YOU CAN DO
Find out what seeps into your groundwater
Take short showers
Recycle at home and at school

A Breath of Fresh Air

Ann Lai

ECO-INVENTOR

"When something goes wrong you can always try to do something about it to make it right. Then you learn something." —Ann Lai

Ann Lai was bored in freshman chemistry class the day her teacher introduced acids and bases. "The teacher was going over the same problem like 15 times, so I started flipping through the textbook," says Ann. A sidebar caught her eye. Acid rain—rain that has become acidic through pollution—is eating away precious historic archi-tecture, such as the Pantheon and Acropolis. Ann was star-tled at the thought of rain devouring stone.

What other harm could acid rain do? Surfing the Web and poring over books at the library, Ann learned how acid rain destroys everything it falls upon, weakening metal, damaging forests, and killing fish and mollusks. Sulfur dioxide from coal burning industries, such as steel mills and paper pulp mills, was the biggest culprit.

She investigated further. "I had to see what's being done to stop acid rain," she says. She found that scientists had developed scrubber systems and neutralization systems to clean up sulfur dioxide. But they had no way to measure how much sulfur dioxide a plant emitted. How could people effectively control sulfur dioxide if they didn't know how much was pouring out? "I really wanted to do something," says Ann. "Sulfur dioxide is a huge problem and we didn't even know how to measure it."

Ann thought she could help find a way. After all, she loved science and research. She delved into articles and books on sensor technology. Perhaps scientists had missed something obvious, she thought. Perhaps a sensor already existed that could measure sulfur dioxide. Maybe it would just take someone like her to notice that a sensor could be used that way. "People might think, 'Yeah, that's a big problem, but you're just a high schooler. What can you do?'" Ann says. "I've always been, like, 'I'm going to do this anyway.'"

Searching through books, Web sites, and science journals, Ann discovered that electrochemical microsensors measure chemicals like carbon monoxide. Maybe they could be adapted to measure sulfur dioxide. A lab at Case Western Reserve University, not far from Ann's home in Beachwood, Ohio, specialized in developing these sensors.

She called C. C. Liu, head of the lab. "I'm a freshman in high school, and I'd like to develop an electrochemical microsensor to measure sulfur dioxide, which contributes to acid rain," Ann said. "May I work at your lab?"

Liu didn't fall off his seat. Instead he asked for a proposal. Ann thought of everything she'd learned about what should be in a proposal. "I knew a strong proposal should include not only what I wanted to do, but why and how," she says. "I can do that." And she did.

Solving the Puzzle

Once scientists in the lab showed Ann how the equipment worked—computers, photosensitive plates, pneumatic printing machines, and rubylith cutters—they were too busy to supervise her, so she was basically on her own. That was okay with Ann—that left her free to test her ideas. Plus, she could always go to C. C. Liu for help. "He was really my mentor," she says.

Designing the sensor was a fascinating puzzle. Should it be circular, elliptical, or rectangular? "The shape of the sensor changes how the sensor operates," Ann says. Many existing sensors are rectangular and they are easy to print, she thought. Semicircular, concentric circular, and concentric elliptical designs would offer more surface area and adjacency between electrodes. She also wanted to try different sizes for each shape to see how size affected the workings of the sensor.

Ann sketched out the possibilities using computer-aided design. "I love art, and designing the sensor combined art and science, so that was fun," she says.

The work was dangerous in many ways. The gases Ann experimented with were poisonous. "I had to be really careful to remember to turn everything off when I switched gases or switched tubes so that nothing actually leaked," she says. She wore goggles and gloves and used protective mitts.

Testing, Testing . . .

Designing a sensor was only the first step. She had to make the sensor and then find out if it would work in the real world. To test a design, Ann exposed the sensor to different levels of sulfur dioxide to see if it could measure the differences. Then, she added other chemicals to see what happened to the sensor's measurement of sulfur dioxide. And she heated and cooled the sensor to see if the temperature changes affected the readings.

Ann tried to design a way to test the sensors at different temperatures using a glass tube. "When it heated up, it exploded," Ann says. "I said to myself: 'Okay, calm down and do this again.'"

In science, sometimes what is easy is hard and what is hard is easy. Take testing, for example. "It was easy because you have to repeat the same thing over and over with only one little change," she says. "But it was really hard because it got really tedious."

Once, when she was testing a sensor, she cranked the heat too high and the plastic covers on the wires melted. Five months of work in one messy lump of plastic. "I freaked out," Ann says. "I'm a very emotional person. But if I can calm myself down quickly, I can actually address the problem faster by finding out what is wrong or what I need to change."

She realized that failures are not failures in science. "When something goes wrong, you can always try to do something about it to make it right," she says. "Then you learn something."

That's how science works. "You have to really be dedicated to research," she says. "When catastrophes happen you have to stick with it and believe that it will work and continue to work on it."

A Scientific Breakthrough

Over the next three years, Ann spent most of her free time at the lab. During the school year, she worked three or four days a week from when school let out until nine or ten at night. She popped into the lab some Saturdays, too.

During the summer, she spent half the week there. "I enjoyed it," she says. "I'd lose track of time."

Ann didn't spend all her time in the lab, though. "When I finished a certain stage or needed a break, I'd go out with friends," Ann says. "I love hanging out and chatting with friends. Plus, then they wouldn't get mad at me or anything."

Her friends were impressed with her work. "They were like: 'Oh my god, I can't believe you are doing this! This is so cool!'" Some even became interested in science research and got involved with experiments at other labs.

After three years of hard work, what did Ann get? A tiny ceramic wafer, very thin, about an inch tall and an inch and a half wide, with patterns printed on it in metal ink. But this little sensor is super adaptable.

The sensor can be placed almost anywhere. "You can put it near the top of a chimney or you can have the air pumped through a pipe and put the sensor there," Ann says. "You can measure continuously the amount of sulfur dioxide emitted over time from a certain smokestack. You can even put it on city street corners, around traffic lights, to see how sulfur dioxide emissions change throughout the day, or stick it in the middle of the forest to see how much sulfur dioxide wafts in."

Ann has applied for a patent for her sensor. Several companies are interested in manufacturing it when the patent comes through. The U.S. Environmental Protection Agency, or EPA, limits how much sulfur dioxide a company can emit, but the agency hasn't been able to measure and enforce their rules—until now. Each sensor costs only $9 to produce, so factories all over the country could use it with little added expense.

"I'm proud that I was able to come up with something like this to protect the environment," she says. "That I actually carried it through and it worked."

What helped her through the hard times was her interest—her passion. "Some people are good at fundraising or creating awareness in the community," Ann says. "Other kids like me are more interested in the scientific aspect." Her advice: "Use your talent on whatever intrigues you the most."

WHAT YOU CAN DO

Take a bike or walk instead of asking for a ride

Research an environmental issue you care about

Plant a tree in your yard or neighborhood park

IDEAS THAT CAN CHANGE THE WORLD

"To convince people to go solar, show them that it works just as well. Build two houses—a coal-, gas-, or oil-powered house next to a solar-powered house so people can come and see."

—Jack Kolb, age 10

"Every child who could afford it could support one endangered animal. I would choose the Bengal Tiger in Asia that the World Wildlife Fund helps. There's also the spider monkey, the collared anteater, the scarlet macaw, and Alaskan caribou. Even the Hawaiian state bird needs help—the Mene Goose." **—Juliet Sohns, age 10**

"I think one of the reasons that the environment is getting destroyed is the carelessness of people. I think someone should invent something that can be built into faucets or light fixtures that can show how much water or energy you have used that day and show what is a good amount to use without hurting the environment." **—Jess Epsten, age 13**

"To fight global warming, we must find an unlimited resource to keep us from overheating. A resource that will go a long time without running out is dark matter. Dark matter consists of the particles between planets and stars, and all the voids throughout the Universe. We should test this idea by sucking dark matter out of space, inventing something to transport it to Earth, and then using it for putting out fires, for cooling homes instead of using air conditioners, and for cooling down the weather." **—Thomas Scharff, age 12**

"We don't need all the stuff that is invented. People who try to invent stuff should think about more than the money they could get out of it; they should start caring about how their invention helps or hurts the planet."

—Stacie Lynae Wilson, age 11

"What if there was an automatic tree planter? Every time you cut down a tree, you would have this unique machine  to plant more trees. You could program it to plant as many seeds as you want. This would be a great machine for loggers to have. It would be a forest saver!" **—Robin Rosecrans, age 11**

YOUR SOLUTION!

Chapter Five

A PLACE TO CALL YOUR OWN

"The ache for home lives in all of us, the safe place where we can go as we are and not be questioned." **—Maya Angelou**

You could never tell by looking at Patrick or talking with him that he is homeless. He's 12 years old and has blond hair and sparkling blue eyes. His favorite activities are gazing at planets through his telescope and playing with his cat Pearl, who can fetch.

"I don't really think of myself as homeless," Patrick told me one night at the Goose Hollow Family Shelter in Portland, Oregon. "I'm out of a home temporarily, or something like that." But that was his sixth night at the shelter, and he, his mom, and his 10-year-old sister Krysta had stayed at another shelter for a whole month.

Teachers and classmates don't realize that Patrick is homeless. "I'm just a normal kid walking around," Patrick says. "The shelters have washing machines and showers and donated clothes and all, so you go to school and you don't even look like a poor kid or anything."

Who Is Homeless?

Some people think all homeless people are dirty, crazy, unemployed drunks and drug addicts. But really there is only one thing that all homeless people share—lack of a place to call their own. Over the course of a year, several million people in American have no place to call home. A quarter of them have jobs. Another quarter are kids. In fact, families with children make up 40 percent of the homeless population, according to the National Coalition for the Homeless.

It's tough to count the exact number of homeless people. Some researchers try counting the number of people staying in shelters one night, but this misses people who crash on the couches of friends and family and those who sleep on the street, in their cars, or in makeshift homes, such as tents.

In most cases, homelessness is temporary—not permanent. So researchers ask all sorts of people if they've been homeless sometime in the last few years. One telephone survey found that 7 percent of Americans have been homeless at some time in their lives—roughly 12 million people!

That means someone you know may have experienced homelessness. Many shelters only house people at night. "The worst is when it's cold outside, and it's raining, and you don't have anywhere to go because the library is closed and all the stores are closed," Patrick says. "You get so cold and wet and all you can do all day is ride the bus back and forth."

What else does it mean to have no home? No home means nowhere to put your clothes and toys. Patrick's prized telescope is stored in his grandmother's basement. "I just really hope I can get it back to watch the next meteor shower," he says.

Homelessness means nowhere to have friends over, nowhere to keep a pet. "Our cat, Pearl, is staying with the vet," says Patrick's sister Krysta. "If we can't get her soon, she'll go to a good family." Homelessness means no phone, TV, or stove to cook a hot meal.

A New Home

You might get some of those things if your family is lucky enough to find space in a housing program, or get help with the rent. But lots of homeless families don't get the help they need from the government. Poor working families must wait an average of two years or more to get housing assistance.

Shelters, many run by volunteers, offer a temporary solution. "There are a couple good things about staying at a shelter," says Patrick's sister Krysta. "You make good friends, you have a bed to sleep in and some food every day, and they really try to take care of you. If you need stamps to write a letter to someone, they will give you some. They will do anything to help."

What follows are the stories of kids who found special ways to help people with no place to call home.

Stand by Me

Kerri Stephen and April Mathews

HOMELESS KID HELPERS

"You can always make something good out of what seems to be a bad experience." **—April Mathews**

"You never realize how much you really have until it's all gone," says April Mathews. When April was 10 years old, she lived outside Washington, D.C. in a big blue house with a huge backyard and a deck, a cat, and a dog. She and her sister Lori had their own rooms and many friends in the neighborhood. Her dad was a systems analyst for the U.S. Department of Defense and earned enough money so the family owned their home.

Then, one October, her dad's drinking got really bad. When he checked himself into rehab for treatment for his alcoholism, the family couldn't keep up with the mortgage payments and the bank foreclosed on the house. They had to move.

At first, April, Lori, and their mom shared a single room at their mom's friend's house. The three found it aggravating to live in such close quarters.

One night, just after New Year's, April's mom announced that they were going to move to a shelter. "At first I was relieved," April recalls. "And then it really hit me. When we spent our first night at the shelter, I sat up most the night and cried: 'Why can't I be normal?'"

The first shelter was a big house where each family shared a room and everyone in the shelter shared two bathrooms, the kitchen, and chores. The shelter had a nice family atmosphere, but the Mathews were only allowed to stay there for two weeks.

April still went to the same school, but she told her friends she was moving to a different neighborhood. When they asked for her phone number, she said she didn't know it yet, or that she couldn't give it out because her parents would get mad. "I only told maybe one or two of my closest friends," April says. "I was so ashamed."

They moved to the Prince William County Homeless Prevention Center, an old one-story motel that had been renovated to a 30-bed shelter by Volunteers of America. The Mathews family lived in a room with their own bathroom, but no kitchen, for three months. Dinner was served in a trailer, called the Mod. Churches took turns preparing meals for the families. April's sister Kayla was born during the time that they lived at the shelter, and April celebrated her eleventh birthday there.

While staying at the shelter, April became friends with Kerri Stephen, the daughter of the director. A few months after the Mathews family moved out of the shelter and into an apartment, April and Kerri were hanging out, talking about AfterShare, a program where formerly homeless adults helped currently homeless adults get back on their feet. AfterShare volunteers gave advice and support and a shoulder to cry on. "We were jealous of the program for adults," says April. "Kids have needs, too."

Homeless Shelter Blues

April and Kerri talked about how living in a shelter is not easy for kids. "You can't spend the night at your friend's house or have them over to yours," says April. "You can't go to the mall and hang out with your friends because you have no money. The only phone is in the hall, so no one can really call you. You spend most of your time in your room with your family. If you're under 12, you can't go anywhere without your parents." Sometimes the food is good, sometimes it's bad, and sometimes you have to eat the same thing every day for a week.

So April, Kerri, April's sister Lori, and Lori's friend Stephanie Conard created AfterShare Kids. First, they drafted a mission statement. They wanted to raise awareness of the plight of the hundreds of thousands of homeless kids, and help kids at the shelter cope. "When you're at the shelter, you don't realize that there are other kids that are going through the same thing," says April. "Even though there are other kids there, you still feel alone."

The foursome recruited kids to volunteer when they moved out of the shelter. The twenty or so AfterShare Kids hung out with kids at the shelter, watching movies with them, painting pottery, and making bracelets. They scraped together money so students could buy their school pictures or join sports teams that charged a fee. They spoke about homelessness at schools. They threw Halloween and Christmas parties at the shelter. And they talked to kids. "You sit down and say, 'I know exactly what you're going through, I went through it, too,'" April says.

One night, a girl who was living at the shelter stepped into the Mod for dinner, only to see one of the "cool girls" from her school, someone who had just started to befriend her, there dishing out food. "She ran back to her room crying," says April. "AfterShare Kids helped her calm down. We told her that it's not the end of the world that she knows you're homeless." They sat the two girls down together and the "cool girl" said: "You know, I don't care if you live here. It's not your fault."

Moving On

April is proud of her work with AfterShare Kids. "I felt like I owed the shelter something because they gave us a place to stay when we needed it," she says. "I wanted to give back."

After a few years, April had to give up volunteering with AfterShare Kids. When her dad found his footing, the family moved out of the apartment in the neighborhood into a town house, and eventually into their own home. Her dad needed her help after he had hip surgery. And she got a job.

Kerri still carries the torch. AfterShare Kids was absorbed into the adult program, which was renamed AfterShare Families and Kids.

"It's tough when kids move out of the area," Kerri says. "It would be great to get some funding for transportation so kids who want to help could come back."

April still believes in the cause and gets offended when she overhears casual remarks like: "Your dad's a bum." "I try not to act on it because I see it as ignorance," she says. "But occasionally I'll say something like 'You know, that's not a very nice thing to say. You could be homeless tomorrow.'" Sometimes she'll admit that she has been homeless. The funny thing is, people often think she's just saying that to make a point or to get attention.

But she wants them to know it's true. "People visualize homeless people as bums you see on the street," April says. "But people from every walk of life, from every race, are homeless. Not all homeless people are drug addicts or alcoholics or anything like that. Homelessness exists in every city, in every town, in every state, in every country."

April doesn't want people to feel sorry for her. "I learned that you can always make something good out of what seems to be a bad experience," she says. "I was like, 'Oh my god, I'm homeless.' I thought it was the worst thing in the world. But if I hadn't been homeless, I wouldn't have been able to help kids and I wouldn't be able to value the things that I have now. It was one of the most eye-opening experiences of my life."

WHAT YOU CAN DO

Hang out with a homeless kid
Volunteer at a shelter
Donate toys and games to a shelter

Mending Lives

Shifra Mincer

SOUP-KITCHEN SEAMSTRESS

"You can use any talent to help other people. If there is anything you like to do, you can help people." —Shifra Mincer

Shifra Mincer never thought she'd spend her Monday afternoons stitching homeless people's clothes. Then one day, her sixth-grade teacher invited kids to help serve food at a soup kitchen in the basement of Hebrew Union College in New York City. As Shifra spooned stew and rice onto plates, someone asked: "Does anyone here know how to sew?"

Sewing is part of the fabric of Shifra's family. One grandmother hand-made all her children's clothes. Her father's parents owned a tailor shop. Her dad, who is handy with a needle, once stitched a ripped baseball mitt.

Her mother repairs the kids' clothes and sews curtains for their apartment. Shifra could sew, too, but she was shy.

"Uhm, yeah, I know how to sew," Shifra said, almost whispering. Someone next to her nudged her: "Say it louder. You can sew."

Shifra shuffled forward, eyes down. "I was very small and timid, so for me it was a big deal to talk up in a crowd," she says. "I was not the type of person to make myself apart from everyone else."

But Shifra said it again: "I can sew."

A volunteer handed her a needle, a thread, and a chair, and announced to the crowd of homeless people gathering around the tables: "If you need anything sewn, bring it here!"

A man removed his jacket and stood over Shifra as she stitched the seam. She sewed a button on a woman's blouse. She mended a hole in another person's pants.

Then word spread through the 150 or so people eating that someone was repairing clothes for free. People huddled around her, holding out their tattered clothes and bags. But the teacher had to get back to school and Shifra had to go with her. "I'm really sorry, I have to go now," Shifra said. "But I promise I'll be back next week."

The next Monday, Shifra returned. "The same thing happened," Shifra says. "Time was up and I really, really had to sew more things and I felt so bad about it." So she returned again and again, staying until 6:30 or 7:00 at night. When her teacher stopped going a few month later, Shifra continued on her own, riding the subway to West 4th Street every week.

Sewing Club

Shifra's work was never done. Every week, new tears and holes needed fixing. Jackets snag or just wear down to loose threads from being used all day and night for months.

"I thought to myself: 'I'll make this like a club,'" says Shifra. "I'll make sure I go every week, just like choir and everything else I was doing after school. By seventh grade, it was just something I had to do because I couldn't leave them without anyone to sew their stuff."

Needing more supplies, Shifra bought buttons, pins, thread of all colors, Velcro, and snaps. These she placed in a red plastic box, ready for use each week.

Now people call her the soup kitchen's Official Seamstress. People on the streets who have heard about the soup kitchen seamstress say: "Oh, you're so little! I expected an old lady to be here sewing." But Shifra knows she can sew as well as any adult. "I realize that I'm capable," she says. "Even though I'm a kid, I can still help—I do a lot."

Most of the homeless people trust Shifra and drop off bags, clothes, and shoes when they arrive and pick them up after they eat. She sews jackets, pants, shirts, and blouses. She'll stitch up a baseball hat and reattach the sole of a shoe. She'll mend worn out bags, taping them together when they are too far gone.

Some people still don't feel safe leaving their few prized possessions, so they watch over Shifra while she works. "I'm used to it now, but at first it made me feel uncomfortable and rushed," she says.

Sweets for the Sweet

Shifra carries the people she meets in her heart all week. When it's raining outside, she thinks of them. When it's hot and humid, she hopes they find somewhere cool to sleep.

"I used to be just so scared of homeless people, so very, very scared. Now, it's so natural for me; they are just people."

She gets small glimpses into the lives of people who live on the streets. One guy had three jobs. "I always had to sew his bags because he's running ragged here and there, back and forth," she says.

Sometimes she sees people in the street wearing the clothes she has mended. "It becomes so real," she says. "These people don't have much to wear and there might have been this huge rip and I sewed it up for them and they're not freezing cold because of that. It makes me really proud."

Plus, the people are just so thankful, Shifra says. "It feels very good when they feel happy that I'm fixing their stuff."

One person offered her candy, saying, "Sweets for the sweet!" An artist has given her small paintings and drawings. Another man used to bring her a small present whenever she sewed for him, a newspaper or some little thing he found. Shifra was sad when she heard he had passed away. "I get to know the regulars," she says. "There are faces that I just know I'll see every week, even if I don't sew for them."

She sews for the man with the humpback, and the fellow who's very, very short and thin. She sews for the woman who is always neatly dressed and clean. She sews

for big guys in leather jackets, and a roller-blader with col-
orful stickers on his helmet. And she sews for the
disheveled men and women who look worn and lost.

A few get too friendly with Shifra. One old man asked
her to run off to Las Vegas with him to get married.

"No, I can't go with you," Shifra said

"We can walk there in five minutes!" he'd say. Or, "I'll
hide you away in my bag!"

Shifra tries not to let experiences like that bother her.

"But for a while, I felt anxious about him coming over,"
she says. "It was unpleasant."

The security guard said he would protect her. Now if
people bother her, she ignores them saying: "I'm working
now." Most of the time, they wander away.

A few take their anger at the world out on Shifra.
They'll say impatiently: "Fix this, fix that."

"This is a very expensive leather jacket. Don't ruin it."

"You didn't do it right!" When she redoes something
they'll grumble: "You finally got it right."

Mostly Shifra stays quiet. She doesn't want to snap
back at them.

She feels bad when she botches a job. Sometimes, she's
rushing to finish all the work piled before her and her
stitching suffers. "Once this guy gave me this look," she
says. A seam she sewed was puckering. "I felt really bad
and I said, 'I'm sorry, I'll take it back, I'll fix it up.' But he
had to go."

Shifra has taken on some really hard projects. "I never
turn down a sewing job," she says. Once, someone gave
her a jacket with all the pockets ripped out. "I found new

material and I made new pockets," she says. "That took some patience, but I didn't give up."

More Than You Put In

Shifra plans to keep sewing all through high school. "I'll feel really sad when we have to find someone to take my place," she says. "I don't want it to be any time soon. I'd miss it a lot."

What's to miss? "It makes me feel so good to come, especially if I'm having a stressful day at school or if I got a bad grade on a test," Shifra says. "When I'm sewing there, I really can't do anything about school. I really have time to completely forget about any problems. And I see people who have a lot more problems than me."

"Volunteering takes a lot of my own time, but you get so much more back," she says. "My life is so different from what it used to be. So much fuller. It was a lot emptier in a way. I'm much more comfortable relating to people, going up to a person I don't know and talking to them. I've become more sensitive to how people are feeling."

"Whatever you put in, you get double back," she says. "It's very hard to explain."

WHAT YOU CAN DO
Ask how to help at a soup kitchen or shelter
Collect blankets and coats for the homeless
Repair donated clothes

IDEAS THAT CAN CHANGE THE WORLD

"Some of the money that is currently being spent on large, costly housing developments should be used to build  homes for those who can't afford a huge house. For every house over a certain size that is built, the developer has to pay a tax to help pay for shelters, medical care, education, and job training for homeless people."

—Abagael West, age 12

"Build shelters in smaller cities that may not have one available. They could use empty buildings that are just going to be demolished or use old schools or old military installations."

—Josh Volpe, age 14

 "Create a special organization or post office so that when homeless people apply for a job they get a free P.O. box so they have an address to put on their application. It could also have answering machines so they could get messages." **—Leah Meijer, age 14**

"People that have millions of dollars could make donations. We could convince them to donate by showing them pictures of people sleeping in cardboard boxes. We could put posters in the areas where wealthy people live. If they see the posters, hopefully they will think of something they can do to help." **—Matthew Thomas, age 10**

"Police should have special training about drug and alcohol rehabilitation centers. That way they could tell homeless people with those problems where to get help."

—Jacob Bocian, age 10

YOUR SOLUTION!

Chapter Six

GET WELL SOON

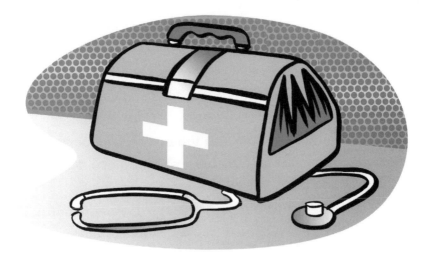

"While the sick have life, there is hope." —Cicero

First you feel a tickle in your nose, scratchiness in your throat. You sneeze, your eyes welling with tears. You grab a tissue. After a few hours, your nose becomes rubbed raw from all the blowing. Your head, too heavy to lift from the pillow, now throbs. One minute, you throw off the blankets, your skin blazing to the touch. The next minute, you pull the covers up to your chin and curl into a ball, shivering.

Your back aches, your head aches, your throat aches, and you're sure no one has ever felt as badly as you do. But sickness is one thing we all face. Everyone gets sick.

But not everyone gets what they need to feel better.

Nearly 40 million Americans—11 million of them kids—don't have any health insurance. If they get sick with something more serious than a cold, they may or may not have enough money to go to a doctor. More than a *billion* people in the world live on less than one dollar a day, each. These people have no access to a doctor, clinic, or hospital—and no money to pay for them if they did.

That's why sicknesses that could be prevented are not. One in four children in the world does not get routine immunizations for diseases like tetanus and measles. Fourteen million people die each year from curable diseases, including malaria and tuberculosis. In many cases, the vaccines or treatments cost less than a dollar per person.

Of course, when you're sick, you need more than just doctors and drugs. You need love and support to get through the pain and discomfort. The care and attention patients get from doctors, nurses, family members, friends, and volunteers can actually speed recovery. New research suggests that feelings of love and appreciation may even improve the beating of your heart.

These kids help people get the treatment and the cheering up they need to get well soon.

The Long Journey

Ryan Tripp

RECORD-BREAKING, LAWNMOWER-DRIVING, ORGAN DONATION ADVOCATE

"I never wanted to quit because I'd be letting myself down, and my family down, and the little girl who needed a liver transplant. No, I don't think I could have quit even if I wanted to."
—**Ryan Tripp**

One summer, 12-year-old Ryan Tripp was out with his dad, a professional landscaper, mowing lawns. Ten miles from their home in Parowan, Utah, their truck broke down.

"I guess we'll have to walk back to town," Ryan's dad said.

"Why don't we just ride the lawnmowers?" Ryan suggested. So they rolled the mowers off the trailer and drove along the shoulder of the freeway toward town.

As they puttered along, Ryan had an idea: "What if we kept going past town and drove all the way to Salt Lake City?"

"What if we went all the way to Washington, D.C.?" his dad said.

"Yeah, what if we drove all the way to Washington, met the President, and mowed the White House lawn!" Ryan said, laughing.

Ryan and his dad were joking, at first. But when they got home, they checked the Guinness Book of World Records and saw a British man had the record for the longest lawnmower ride: 3,034 miles.

"Let's do this thing," they said. "Let's break this record. It'll be fun!"

Riding for a Reason

Ryan's dad began to plot the route. "People thought we had to get permission from different states to ride on the roads, but we didn't," Ryan says. But they did have to find sponsors to donate a lawnmower hardy enough to make the trip and to help pay for gas, food, and lodging.

Walker Manufacturing donated two mowers, one for Ryan to ride and the other for spare parts. They traded the small tires for road tires. And for visibility, they attached an orange flag and flashing lights. Guinness wouldn't let them do anything else to soup up the lawnmower.

But while swept up in excitement for the trip, Ryan learned some sad news: a four-month-old baby in their town, Whitnie Pender, desperately needed a liver transplant. Transplants can cost thousands of dollars. "I thought, 'Well, she needs a liver transplant and we're going on this trip across America. Wouldn't that be a good way to raise money?'" says Ryan.

The Tripps opened a special bank account for Whitnie. Ryan posted huge signs on the trailer telling people where to send donations for the transplant.

They're Off!

In August, Ryan began his long, slow journey from Salt Lake City. His Grandma and Grandpa drove in front. Then came Ryan on the mower, wearing a helmet and an earplug for a walkie talkie. Ryan's dad took the rear with the truck and trailer.

Day Four was the hardest. "I was just way tired and it was hot and the road went straight through the desert," Ryan says. His dad noticed that the lawnmower was drifting away from the shoulder and onto the road. He honked his horn, but Ryan continued to veer into danger. So his dad maneuvered alongside him and hollered. Ryan had fallen asleep. They pulled over and went right to a hotel.

"I was just getting used to being on a lawnmower all day," says Ryan. "I'd been out all summer playing basketball and being active and all of a sudden, I'm sitting on a lawnmower. It just made me sleepy."

Eventually, the convoy found a rhythm. They'd be up by 7:00, eat breakfast, and ride until lunch. Often, they'd pull the lawnmower up to a drive-thru for lunch.

"We ate so much McDonald's that I can't stand it anymore," Ryan says.

For about 10 hours a day, the lawnmower chugged along, no faster than 10 miles an hour. Distances that took Ryan a full day could have been covered in a car in about an hour and a half! "I just sat there and thought about things," he says. "I listened to my music, and just looked around at the scenery, waving at people driving by. I thought about what I was doing, setting a record and raising money for Whitnie."

To get the record-breaking mileage, Ryan drove clear up to Maine and back down to Washington, D.C. Rain only fell on Ryan for a total of five days. He just donned a raincoat and kept on going. Rain was nothing compared with the monotony of the long days. "I love playing sports and doing stuff with my friends, so sitting all alone on my lawnmower was pretty tough," Ryan says. "I never thought of quitting, but sometimes I'd dwell on how hard it was. I'd be like, 'Oh man, this is just so hard, this sucks.' But I never wanted to quit because I'd be letting myself down, and my family down, and the little girl who needed a liver transplant. No, I don't think I could have quit even if I wanted to."

Ending the Wait

To get people interested in the effort and Whitnie's plight, the Tripps would call ahead to a TV station in the town where they were headed. Sometimes crowds of people would gather there to meet him. When Ryan was interviewed, he'd tell them about the need for organ and tissue donations.

Every day, he explained, 17 people die while waiting for an organ donation. That's about half the students in a typical classroom. More than 65,000 people are on waiting lists for transplants. Because doctors can transplant your heart, kidneys, pancreas, lungs, liver, and intestines, each person who becomes a donor can save up to eight lives.

News of the journey spread faster than the lawnmower could move. "People just handed up money on the side of the road," Ryan says. "I'd be going along and some lady would run up to me and give me ten bucks or whatever."

After driving 3,116 miles, through 19 states, the convoy rolled into Washington, D.C. Ryan mowed the Capitol lawn then headed home. "It was the best day and the worst day," Ryan says. "Seeing all the family I hadn't seen for 42 days, seeing Whitnie Pender and giving her family the money for the liver transplant, setting the world record. But we had to stop a trip that was so fun, you know?"

Ryan raised $15,000 for Whitnie. "She got her liver transplant and she's way good now," Ryan says.

On the Road Again

Ryan was so amazed at Whitnie's recovery that he wanted to bring the organ and tissue donation message to people in all 50 states. He also had his eye on a new world record. So, two years later, he set out again—this time to mow the lawns of all 50 state capitols.

To drive a lawnmower to every state in the country would take years. So the Tripp family towed a trailer for the lawnmower behind a motor home from state to state.

And the mowing wasn't too tough, either. "People thought I had to mow the whole capitol lawn, but Guinness World Records said I only had to mow 1,000 square feet," Ryan says.

When they arrived at a capitol, the Governor or some other official would meet them. Ryan thanked them for greeting him and gave the officials shirts that said: "Ryan's Trip To End The Wait." He also handed them a cup of Lifesavers candy, signifying the lives that could be saved by becoming a donor. Then he'd start to mow.

"In Atlanta, there were about 500 people and ten TV cameras," he says. "It was kind of scary mowing the lawn with all those people watching. You didn't want to scalp the lawn or anything."

He had no trouble compared with the governors and other officials who wanted to mow the lawn with him. "A lot of them didn't know how to ride a lawnmower," Ryan says. "I'd show them how, but they'd run into trees and stuff and just be all over the place, up on sidewalks and down the stairs or whatever. It was crazy!"

Ryan accomplished a big goal on this trip. When he'd ridden across the country, he'd had his heart set on mowing the White House lawn. But the security officials wouldn't let him. Ryan tried again. "We kept pursuing it and talking with people at the White House and it ended up happening," Ryan says. "If something doesn't work out at first, just keep trying. I really believe you can do whatever you put your mind to."

A New Life

Along the way, Ryan met with the families of people who had died and donated their organs. In Tennessee, a donor family gave him a picture of their 17-year-old son playing soccer, with a poem and a note saying: "Thank you Ryan for promoting organ donation. Our son died at age 19 and he donated his organs to save other people's lives."

"That was really cool," Ryan says.

And he met people who were saved by an organ transplant. They told him how hard it was to wait years for a kidney or a lung. How they feared they would die before one became available. How the organ donation gave them a new life.

Ryan has no idea how many people have become organ donors because of his efforts or how many lives he may have saved. In fact, he thinks he's the person who got the most from the trips.

"I grew so much," he says. "I always like to take the easy road. But it wasn't easy to ride across America. But I just kept in mind that I needed to raise money for this little girl, raise awareness, and set the world record. I could've taken the easy road and quit, but I stuck with it, and it was hard, but I got through it."

WHAT YOU CAN DO
Become an organ donor
Encourage people to become organ donors
Throw a fundraiser for a health cause

Hair Today, Gone Tomorrow

Kristel Fritz

HAIR-DRIVE COORDINATOR

"Giving sick kids pride and confidence in themselves was just an awesome, awesome idea." **—Kristel Fritz**

One night, Kristel Fritz flicked on the news and saw a strange sight: Miss Kentucky, wearing a smart suit and sash, posed in a hairdresser's chair. Her golden crown was perched not on her head, but on the cutting station. The hairdresser raised some long shears to Miss Kentucky's head, smiled, and chopped off her long brown hair. Miss Kentucky donated her hair to Locks of Love, an organization that gives kids with medical hair loss custom-fitted wigs.

"The image stayed in my brain when I went to bed," Kristel says.

The next day, Kristel couldn't stop thinking about what an esteem-booster a wig must be for kids who have lost their hair. "In my family, there's a line of women with thinning hair and I've seen their struggle with dealing with not having a lot of hair," she says. "Giving sick kids pride and confidence in themselves was just an awesome, awesome idea."

After reading more on the Web site for Locks of Love, Kristel knew she wanted to contribute to the cause. She learned that two million kids suffer from alopecia areata (al-oh-PEE-shah air-ee-AH-tah), a disease that causes hair loss. She read stories of children who donated hair and stories of kids who received the hair. "Their courage was so inspiring, I really wanted to help in whatever way I could." Long hair was all the rage in Pioneer High School in San Jose, California, where Kristel was a junior. "I thought, 'If I have a hair drive, I'll get so much hair!'" she says.

Down to Business

First Kristel talked to a teacher who said: "Go for it!" Kristel's mom works at SuperCuts and offered to volunteer her time and recruit a couple of her colleagues for a hair drive.

Then Kristel had to get approval from the principal, sign up for the cafeteria with the assistant principal, talk to the event committee of the student body, and make permission forms for the parents of kids under the age of 18.

She hung posters and handed out fliers and wrote an announcement to be read over the loudspeaker during homeroom. One friend made buttons that said: "Locks of Love, ask me for more information."

Kristel started talking it up to classmates. "Kids didn't

want to commit," she says. "People were extremely skeptical because no one had heard of donating hair. They said:
'Hmmm, that's really strange.'" Some kids actually said:
"No way, I'm not going to donate my hair. No, I don't
believe in this cause."

"At first I thought maybe I didn't explain myself completely," says Kristel. "I'd go through the whole spiel
again, giving them statistics and facts thinking that if I
bombarded them with enough information, they'd soon
come over to my side. I was so adamant and passionate
about the cause."

But that didn't work. "Slowly I began to realize that I
could not force kids to change their minds," she says. "It
was hard to realize some people did need to think it over,
and to give them the space to say: 'Yes, I do want to
donate my hair' or even 'No, I don't want to donate my
hair.' I had to learn to be really open to whatever their
decision was and be really positive."

But still, she couldn't help being worried. She had created a vision in her head, where everyone would happily
donate. When kids didn't respond the way she'd hoped,
she thought: "Am I going to get this to fly? Will I get more
than three people to donate hair?"

Only 15 students signed up in advance. "I was actually,
honestly, really disappointed," she says. "The school has
1,200 kids and I was hoping I'd get at least 50."

Making the Cut

On the day of the hair drive, Kristel lugged in five tables
and found five tall chairs from a science lab. She brought
in extension cords from home and a broom and a dustpan
for cleaning up. SuperCuts let the hair cutters borrow

squirt bottles, scissors, clips, and capes from their store.

That day, someone was playing loud techno music in the center quad at lunch. "I thought it would ruin the entire event," Kristel says. "My mom normally listens to country music so I thought she'd hate it." But the music gave the cafeteria a fashion show feel. "The ladies really loved it," Kristel says. "They were dancing and cutting, it was a great sight."

A student would take a seat in the tall chair. "How short do you want your hair after you donate?" the hair-dresser would ask.

She'd put a rubber band at the place the student indi-cated. Then she'd take her scissors and just chop right across. "I'd give the pony tail to the person donating so they could have their parting words with their hair, or whatever," says Kristel.

Then, the surprise: Tears began to flow. "One thing I hadn't anticipated was all the crying," Kristel says. "Every-body, it seemed, was crying. It's hard for teenagers to part with their hair. Hair is part of their identity, who they are."

The Associated Student Body President had agreed to donate. "She had this long, long black hair, below her waist," says Kristel. "Gorgeous and as straight as can be. She always had it pulled back in a bun or ponytail if it wasn't loose and blowing in the wind."

On the day of the drive, the buzz at school was: Would she really do it? Students poured into the cafeteria to watch.

She did it. She had her hair cut to just an inch below her ears. This time the tears came not just from kids who donated hair. Friends stood there watching, crying. Kristel started to worry. What if kids regretted their decision?

What if they talked badly about the hair drive? What if they told people: "Don't go, don't cut your hair."

She tried to really respect their feelings. "I'd just walk over and hold their hand while they were getting their hair cut or just sit there and listen to them," Kristel says. "Really, I just tried to give them whatever they needed."

One girl had a friend with alopecia areata. She was thinking about her friend and how Locks of Love helps kids like her friend. She'd always wanted to donate her hair but she'd never had the courage to cut it all off. "I was really proud that I created this drive, this forum, this space for her to donate her hair," Kristel says.

Five girls were inspired by what their friend did and decided to donate on the spot. They called their parents for permission and got a slip from the school secretary confirming that it was okay.

A man from Berkeley who read about the drive on the Locks of Love Web site brought a ponytail from a friend in Davis, California. A couple, both with long hair, wandered in off the street to donate. The woman carried a ponytail she had saved *and* she offered the hair on her head. The man's hair was curly, and down to the middle of his back. He hadn't cut it for 20 years, since he'd left the Navy. "My mom cut it short, a standard business cut," says Kristel. "It took years off him!"

Kristel collected 25 ponytails in all.

Bags of Hair

After the drive, Kristel swept up and headed to her sixth-period Spanish class. She had nowhere to put the hair, so she took it with her—plastic ziplock baggies of hair over-flowing a paper sack. "All the kids freaked out at the idea of having all that hair there," she says.

Her dad's reaction was even funnier. Kristel had left the paper bag on the kitchen table. When her dad got home, he peeked inside. "He freaked out when he saw the ropes of blonde, black, and red hair. He made me put it in the garage. He was adamant that I could not bring it in the house."

Kristel had to mail the hair to Locks of Love. At the post office, she didn't know what to write on the box. "Fragile"? "Perishable"? She decided on: "Please don't crush or bend." And she wanted it insured. A clerk helped her fill in the form: "What is in the box?" she asked.

"Hair," Kristel said.

"The woman just stopped and looked up and her eyes were so wide and her face just said: Oh my God!" Kristel's mom had to explain, fast: "It's nothing terrible. She's not a scary child or anything. It's a legitimate thing!"

Just Another Ponytail

That night, Kristel confessed to a friend her disappointment at only collecting 25 ponytails. Her friend said: "Yeah, you didn't reach 50, but you got 25 people to do something they never would have done. You gave them the opportunity to do this amazing thing!"

After that, Kristel thought, next year there would be more, and the year after, and the year after. "Things may not have gone the way I'd planned in my mind, but I started the seed for change and it will grow," says Kristel.

The second year all the negativity was gone. "I'm most proud that I was able to effect change on my high school campus," she says. "So many kids heard about it, knew someone who had donated. They really understood it more."

The first year Kristel had run herself ragged coordinating the drive herself. The second year she enlisted the help of six pals. "Reach out to your friends," Kristel says. "Really reach out. Doing something like this can be really overwhelming."

The second year, 30 people donated—five of them guys. One senior, a guy who played in all the school bands, was known for his long hair. Kristel had tried the first year to convince him to donate. "I'll never do it," he said. But the day of the drive, he wandered into the cutting room. He was so moved by the other students' donations that he just sat down in one of the chairs and said: "I want to donate my hair."

And Kristel donated her hair, too. The first year, her hair was way too short. "I thought it would be this huge deal for me because I started the drive," says Kristel. "I just held my ponytail and I thought I'd be overcome with all these emotions. But to me, it was just another ponytail. It was just hair. I just had to smile, knowing it would end up on someone else's head."

WHAT YOU CAN DO

Donate your hair or run a hair drive
Visit sick people to cheer them up
Volunteer at a hospital or nursing home

IDEAS THAT CAN CHANGE THE WORLD

"We should make fast-food restaurants into fruit stands. The restaurants should sell carrots, and apples, and salads, oranges, peaches, and peppers instead of french fries. That might encourage people to eat better. People would try the fruit and realize how great it tastes."

—Roger Peterson, age 11

"We should educate people more about how to take care of themselves—many people don't know anything about health and how to prevent diseases. We should have big conferences in neighborhoods on health care issues, or have people go door-to-door teaching about health care."

—Mai Truong, age 16

"I notice that some doctors rush so they can fit a lot of people in. If they slow down, the appointments will go better and people will be more healthy."

—Alexandria O'Neil, age 13

"In my neighborhood, people have to wait a long time to see a doctor. There should be more small health centers in neighborhoods, so it is easier for *people to get to the doctor and so the doctors are more part of the community."* **—Aaron Garcia, age 15**

"People should get checkups more often, because if something happens that is serious, you have a better chance of surviving if you catch it early. At least every month, just to make sure. Better safe than sorry."
—Christopher Cucinotto, age 13

"Instead of making more freeways just for people to buy cars and ruin our environment, we should use that money and make hospitals and clinics, because those are the things we need the most." **—Verónica Mireles, age 16**

YOUR SOLUTION!

Chapter Seven

THE FACE OF FAIRNESS

"Injustice anywhere is a threat to justice everywhere."
—Martin Luther King, Jr.

*A*re your eyes blue or brown? What if your teacher decides she can tell what kind of student you are based only on your eye color? Because of your eye color, you are told you are not as smart as other kids, not as likable as other kids. No matter how hard you try, the highest grade you can get is a C, because of the color of your eyes.

And it gets worse. Your seat is moved to the back of the class. You must sign out and be accompanied by another student to go to the bathroom. You have to carry an identification card with you to class, in the halls, at lunch, even at recess.

That's the kind of treatment students at Community Elementary School in Riceville, Iowa, experienced during Discrimination Day. Their teacher, Jane Elliott, wanted her white middle-class students to experience what discrimination is like—to suffer the insults, inconveniences, fears, and self-doubt that African-Americans, Arab-Americans, Jews, and other minority groups have faced throughout our country's history.

"Brown Eyes Are Better"

The teacher divided her class into blue-eyed and brown-eyed students. One day she treated the blue-eyed children as if they were inferior, restricting their recess time and their use of the slide, swings, and water fountain. She told the brown-eyed kids that they were better than the blue-eyed kids. When a brown–eyed child stumbled, she helped him. When a blue-eyed child had trouble reading, she looked disgusted and called on a brown-eyed child to read the passage correctly.

A funny thing happened—the brown-eyed students acted as if they really believed they were better than the other kids. They sat up straighter in their chairs, they smiled more, they answered questions in class more easily. They didn't invite blue-eyed kids, even their best friends, to play with them. Blue-eyed children frowned, fidgeted, and fumbled. "Their posture, their expressions, their entire attitudes were those of defeat," said the teacher. "Their classroom work regressed sharply from that of the day before. Inside of an hour or so, they looked and acted as though they were, in fact, inferior. It was shocking."

The next day, the teacher pulled a switcheroo. She told the class that she'd had it all wrong the day before: actually, brown-eyed people are inferior and blue-eyed people superior. That way, both brown-eyed and blue-eyed kids felt the pain of discrimination.

Color Doesn't Matter!

When the teacher reenacted the exercise the next year, the pattern played out again, with an exception. One boy insisted that eye color made no difference in people. "It's not true," he said whenever the teacher made a discriminatory statement. "That's not fair," he said when she made unequal rules.

This boy bucked the trend. He stuck with what he knew was right, even when his teacher told him differently.

What follows are the stories and ideas of other kids who took a stand when they saw people being treated unfairly because of the color of their skin, their culture, the way they dress, their gender, their language, their religion, or for any reason at all.

Biking While Black

Charlie King, Jr. and Davon King

RACIAL PROFILING PLAINTIFFS

"If officers stop one race, they should stop all races."
—Davon King

When Davon King was 12, his bike meant the world to him. A birthday present from his parents, the bicycle was a red and black 15-speed, 24-inch mountain bike, a Roadmaster with white-wall tires and black handle grips.

"That bike took me everywhere," he says. He rode to friends' houses, to the mall, to Burger King, and to visit his grandparents. "Sometimes I'd be tired and I'd need to go somewhere and I'd think, 'Man, I do not feel like riding today.' But once I got going, I'd always enjoy it."

Since moving from a mostly black neighborhood in Detroit to Eastpointe, a mostly white suburb, Davon, an

African-American, sometimes felt self-conscious. "Some people would be shocked to see an African-American," he says. "When I rode by, they'd just stare at me." But that didn't really bother Davon. In the summer of 1995, he mostly felt free.

Then, one afternoon, Davon and his older brother Charlie (then 14) were biking to Farmer Jack's, a grocery store near their house. They were pedaling and talking when a police car drove up next to them. The officer yelled out the window: "Stop and get off your bike."

Startled, they did.

The exchange, according to Davon, went something like this:

"Black kids are stealing bikes in Eastpointe and taking them to Detroit," the officer said. "What are your names?"

"Davon King"

"Charlie King."

"Do you have any ID?"

"No," the boys answered.

"Why aren't you in school?" the officer asked.

"It's summer."

The officer asked for their address and where they went to school. "Are these bikes registered?"

The boys looked at each other and shrugged. "I don't know," Charlie answered. "You'd have to ask our dad."

"That's okay," the officer said. "I'm not accusing you of anything. I just wanted to make sure you were on your own bikes." And he told them they could go. The boys thought nothing of it.

Black Biker, White Biker

Then, a few weeks later, Davon and Charlie were riding

their bikes to the K-Mart in Eastpointe. A police car passed by. The brothers pedaled on. As they turned down a street, the police car pulled into a driveway, turned around and headed back to them—with the siren screaming and lights flashing. There were two police officers this time. "Stop!" one yelled. "Get off your bikes."

As the boys swung their legs over the bike seats, both officers got out of the car. One asked Charlie for his name, address, and school. Charlie told him.

Then the officer turned to Davon.

Davon remembers how he felt at that moment: "I was nervous because a cop had stopped me," he says. "I hadn't done anything, I thought, so why is he stopping me?"

The officer asked for his name.

"I told him, he said he didn't hear me, so I repeated it," Davon recalls. "He said he didn't hear me again, so I repeated it louder. He kept on saying he didn't hear me. So my brother said my name. Then the cop said: 'I didn't ask you, smart guy.' He wanted me to repeat my name one more time, so I did."

Some bikes had been stolen, the officer told them. But while Davon and Charlie were detained, a white kid rode by on a bike, and the police officers didn't stop him.

"I was mad," Davon says. "This Caucasian kid rolled right in front of the cops and neither officer did anything to stop him. They didn't say: 'Hey, wait, stop for a minute. Can you come over here for a minute?' For all they knew he could have been stealing that bike and taking it to Detroit."

Again, the officer asked the boys for the registration for their bikes. Again the boys said to ask their father. And the officer said they could go.

This time, Davon and Charlie told their parents. The King family decided that, to be on the safe side, the boys should ride their bikes less often—only a couple times a month. "My dad was afraid that the police officers would do something more severe," Davon says.

The Last Straw

One day the next spring, the brothers had a half day at school. They called their mom at work for permission to ride their bikes to get a snack. They stopped first at Burger King, but the lines were long, so they pedaled over to Arby's. Charlie waited with the bikes while Davon went in. While he was deciding what to order, he noticed that his money wasn't in his pocket.

"Let's go back and retrace our steps," Charlie suggested.

As they pedaled slowly back, a police car pulled up beside them. The officer yelled out the window for them to stop. Davon and Charlie pulled into the adjacent parking lot and straddled their bikes.

"Get off and lean your bikes on the light post," the officer commanded as he climbed out of his car.

The officer asked for ID. When the boys said they didn't have any, he said: "Why don't they give ID cards at your school?"

Charlie answered: "Because it's a middle school."

The officer asked them a bunch of questions: Why aren't you in school? Where are your parents? Why didn't you buy anything from the restaurants you stopped in?

The officer grabbed Charlie by the arm and put his hands on the trunk of the car while he patted him down. When Davon recalls what happened next, his voice deepens with anger. "He yanked Charlie's pants up his crotch and pushed him into the backseat of the car."

"What are you going to do to my brother?" Davon asked.

"Do you see him in handcuffs, boy?" the officer said. Another officer arrived on the scene, talked with the first officer, then walked up to Davon. "We'll be in contact with your parents," he said. "Well, y'all are free to go."

"As we pedaled away, I turned around to see what they were doing and they were laughing at us and waving," Davon says. "I thought, 'Why me? What have I ever done to deserve this?'"

Time for Action

The boys again told their parents what happened. But this time, that wasn't enough. "It's not fair that my civil rights have been violated," Davon says. "Caucasian kids can ride bikes up and down the street and have fun and African-American kids should be able to ride up and down and have fun. If officers stop one race, they should stop all races."

That's why Davon grabbed at the chance when his dad said they could file a lawsuit against the city. "I hoped the lawsuit would accomplish justice," Davon says.

So the King family filed two suits, in the summer and fall of 1998. Working for change through the courts is not as glamorous as it seems on TV or in the movies. In fact, though the cases have spanned several years, Davon has never seen the inside of a courtroom. That's because most of the work in a court case happens behind the scenes with lawyers looking for evidence, interviewing witnesses, and scouring documents.

The most dramatic and scary part of the case, Davon says, was when he was deposed. Being deposed means the lawyer for the other side interviews you to find evidence to use against your case. Davon's deposition happened at a big table in a conference room in a high-rise office building. "We went over what happened, how we felt about what happened," he says. "It was very repetitive. They wanted me to remember intricate details about stuff that happened years ago!"

Small Cases, Big Consequences

When Rosa Parks refused to surrender her seat to a white passenger on a bus in Montgomery, Alabama in 1955, she did a simple thing, but it started something big. Her actions kicked off a yearlong boycott of Montgomery buses. And she launched a lawsuit that she lost several times before the U.S. Supreme Court agreed that laws segregating buses were unconstitutional.

In a way, Davon and Charlie's story is similar. One of their cases settled out of court and the boys received a small amount of money. And the other case was dismissed because the judge thought the officers acted reasonably. The Kings are appealing.

But that's just the beginning. While poring over police logs and reports, the Kings' lawyer, Chuck Chomet, found a startling pattern: Between 1995 and 1998, more than 100 African-American kids between the ages of 11 and 18 were stopped by police while riding their bikes in Eastpointe. Some of the young people were searched or handcuffed before being released. Some of the kids' bikes were seized by police and never returned. During the same period, police stopped only 40 white males on bikes, though the area is predominantly white.

When word about the King case got out, from newspaper stories and talk in the neighborhood, African-American families contacted Chomet to see if they could join the case. The lawyer tried to make the Kings' suit into a class action so the court would rule on the pattern of incidents. But the judge wouldn't allow it.

So in August of 2000, Chomet filed another case against Eastpointe police on behalf of 21 African-American kids who were stopped by police while riding their bikes. Eight months later, the American Civil Liberties Union (ACLU) of Michigan joined the lawsuit, adding clout and more lawyer-power.

The case is supported by a memo from the Chief of Police in response to a letter Charlie and Davon's dad sent to the mayor complaining about racial profiling. The police chief defended the practice of police officers stopping black kids on bikes. In the summer of 1995, there had been several complaints of bikes being stolen by young black males, he wrote. "My instructions to the officers were to investigate any black youth riding through our subdivision."

Your Rights

Does the fact that some black kids may have stolen bikes give police officers the right to stop any black kid riding a bike? The Kings' lawyer says no. The Fourth Amendment to the Constitution bars police from unreasonable searches and seizures. That means the police cannot stop and search you and take any of your possessions without reasonable suspicion that a crime was committed and that you were involved.

For each incident, lawyers for Eastpointe will argue that the kids weren't really stopped—they were free to go at any time. Or they'll try to prove that the police had good reason to stop them and they did not intrude any more than necessary to conduct an investigation of a specific crime.

Chomet will argue that the kids were stopped because they were black, that they did not feel free to go, and that the police overstepped their bounds by patting down and handcuffing some of the kids and confiscating their bikes.

An End to Racial Profiling

For the discrimination and humiliation they suffered, the plaintiffs request payment of one million dollars for each party in the case. But they also want an end to racial profiling of kids on bikes in Eastpointe. They want a clear, written policy describing the circumstances under which kids with bikes can be stopped. They want all police officers fully trained on the policy and related constitutional issues. They want information gathered about every case in which African-Americans with bicycles are stopped, and someone to review the incidents to make sure all stops are justified. Finally, they want a way for kids and their families to complain when they think that their constitutional rights have been violated.

"I'm proud that me and my family have been able to motivate people to do something about racial profiling in Eastpointe," Davon says. "I'm proud that my family is an example to other families and that they will be heard just like we have been heard."

WHAT YOU CAN DO

Read the Constitution

Learn more about racial profiling

Plan a bike rally for a cause you care about

Speak Out

Sol Kelley-Jones

EQUAL-RIGHTS ACTIVIST

"The Constitution says that all people are created equal. It does not say all people except gays and lesbians, or all people except for women, or all people except for people of color. It says all people." —**Sol Kelley-Jones**

When Sol Kelley-Jones was 10, a state legislator asked her to testify against AB-104, a bill before the Wisconsin State legislature to ban gay marriage. "Gay marriage was already banned, so its real purpose was to perpetuate hate," says Sol, pronounced "soul." The hearing was moved out of Madison, the capital, and up north to the small town of Wassau. Conservative committee members scheduled the hearing on a Monday, a workday. Still, 12 busloads of people opposing the bill made the trip.

The sky that March day was a cold but brilliant blue.

Sol stood between her two mothers, Joann Kelley and Sunshine Jones, holding their hands. The family pushed through the hearing room doors into a crowd of more than 500 people. Engulfed by the crowd and flashing cameras, Sol was scared. Some people shoved cameras in her face saying: "Now we'll know who you are."

"Mom, what are they going to do with those pictures?" Sol asked.

"I don't know. It'll be okay. Hold your head up high," her mom said, almost in tears. People held up signs stating: "God hates homosexuals." Others called her parents sinners. One speaker even suggested that gay people be put to death. At the beginning of the hearing, a witness for the bill said that gay and lesbian couples marrying is like a person marrying a horse.

"It was really frightening," Sol says. "Anything could happen. It was very congested. There was this feeling of hate in the air and they were all around you."

The World Stops

Then Sol sat down to testify. "As soon as I spoke, everything came from deep within me," she says. "It was like this moment where everything seemed to stop. It felt so right that I wasn't scared anymore." This is what she said:

Hi, my name is Sol Kelley-Jones. I am ten years old. I'm a really lucky kid because I have two parents who love each other and love me very much. My parents are always helping me and lots of other people, too. My friends tell me how lucky I am because I have always had a mom at home with me after school, who fixes great snacks.

Not everyone is lucky enough to have two great parents, so I know I have a lot to be thankful for. Some people don't understand everything about my family—like having two moms.

They ask me: "Who is your real mom?" I say: "They're both my real moms." I have a great family full of lots of love. That's why it's hard for me to understand why people are so afraid of us that they want bills like this. I don't see any way that this bill helps families, and it hurts my family a lot.

After speaking for about three minutes, Sol finished her testimony. No one was supposed to applaud. "I stopped and looked up and heard this roar of clapping," Sol says. Despite Sol's efforts, the bill passed in the committee.

"That could be considered a failure," Sol says, "but it really wasn't because I learned to find my own voice and trust what I have to say in my heart, even when it's really scary." A legislator told Sol afterward that she voted against the bill because of Sol's testimony.

Speaking from the Heart

Since then, Sol has testified about a dozen times, before Wisconsin State legislative committees, the Madison city council, and the local school board. She has spoken on issues such as health insurance benefits for gay families, domestic partnership, second parent adoption, and school harassment.

"I try to listen and say what is in my heart," she says. A history buff, she also sprinkles in people and stories from the Revolutionary War, the civil rights movement, and the Constitution. "The Constitution says that all people are created equal," she says. "It does not say all people except gays and lesbians, or all people except for women, or all people except for people of color. It says *all* people."

At age 10, Sol told the story of Elizabeth Freeman, a black woman who, before the Revolutionary War, was owned by one of the authors of the Constitution. According to Sol:

As a slave, she didn't have any rights. Elizabeth Freeman couldn't get legally married, and her kids could get taken away from her. Today, my parents also can't get legally married, and it's scary for me to know that if one of my parents died, I could be taken away from my other parent. Two hundred years ago, Elizabeth Freeman went to the government and asked for her rights—like it said in the Constitution.

Some people hated or feared African-Americans so much that they would have changed the Constitution rather than allow Elizabeth Freeman her rights. They said terrible things, like if African-American people were freed and had equality under law, everything Americans believed in would crumble. Elizabeth Freeman won her freedom, the right to legally marry and to protect her children. And America didn't crumble, it got better.

Like African-American kids who withstood taunts and threats, and integrated schools in Little Rock, Arkansas, Sol refuses to let her age stop her from speaking out against that unfairness. "Youth are totally on the front lines of every single movement in history," she says. "We've always been there and we always will be."

Tough Times

Sol has suffered from discrimination and harassment, too. When registering for kindergarten, Sol couldn't understand why the school insisted on listing one of her moms as "a friend of the family" instead of as a parent.

In fourth grade, when Hawaii was considering allowing gay marriage, Sol clipped articles for her teacher to staple on the current events bulletin board. "He didn't put the articles up," she says. "He put up all the other kids' articles." At first she thought he lost them and was too embarrassed to tell her. So she submitted them again. "I kept making excuses for him, but he never put them up, and he never said anything to me," she says. "Sometimes that silence—that silent homophobia, that silent racism, that silent classism—hurts the most."

Sol surveyed 101 students at her school on their attitudes toward gay and lesbian people. Forty percent said they wouldn't play with a kid if they found out he or she had gay or lesbian parents. "That was really hard to hear," Sol says, "but I was totally determined to make a difference about it." The next year she designed a project to educate kids about homophobia. She wanted to survey kids before and after a multimedia presentation about how homophobic words hurt, myths about homosexuals, and famous gay and lesbian people. She wanted to play Elton John's music, read Langston Hughes' poetry, and discuss Jane Addams, the founder of social work. The teacher wouldn't let her do it unless the parents of all the students in the class signed permission slips. "Requiring permission slips sent a message that there was something wrong about seeing families like mine and learning about people in the culture I grew up in," she says.

With the help of a gay teacher and her mom, she found five teachers who invited Sol to present in their classrooms. "Kids in my class would have been totally fine," Sol says. "They were excited about it. When I presented in another classroom, they came and peeked their heads through the door because they wanted to see it." Sol held out hope that her teacher would relent. "I held on to all these books from the library until the very last week," she says, "but he wouldn't let me present."

Huge Wave of Hate

In middle school, the harassment got worse. "I walked into the first day of sixth grade, and I was just totally taken aback by this huge wave of hateful, cruel words," she says. "I was overwhelmed. I didn't know what to do. It just seemed so big, and the teachers did nothing to stop it. It was depressing."

One day, she counted hearing homophobic slurs, such as faggot, fruit, gaywad, or homo, 34 times before 11:00 AM. It didn't matter whether the targeted person was gay or not. It was simply an insult that kids could get away with at school.

Sol wore a rainbow necklace to school and a rainbow ribbon on her backpack, symbols of gay pride and diversity. She wanted gay kids or kids from gay families to know they were not alone. Students picked on her for it. They'd say, "Oh, what are you? Some kind of fag lover?" Sol tried to talk with them about it. "C'mon, that's not cool," she'd say.

The harassment got worse. Students called her a faggot, wrote homophobic epithets on her student council posters, and tripped her down the stairs.

Sol transferred in the middle of seventh grade. "I really wanted to stay," says Sol. "I had my friends there, and I wanted to do something to change the climate. I had all these ideas on ways to educate kids. But school staff didn't feel they could keep me safe there."

Sol forged ahead with her education efforts in her new school. In an English class where students had to give oral reports about different cultures, Sol did a presentation on gay culture. But when she announced her topic, the room went completely silent. "You know how middle schoolers are never quiet," she says. "Well, you could hear a pin drop. It was very intimidating at first. But I got up there and did my presentation, and after a while they overcame their nervousness and totally listened." Afterward, some students thanked her for doing the presentation.

An Unexpected Ally

But the real payoff came later, in history class. They were studying the Fourteenth Amendment to the Constitution, the Equal Protection Clause, which prohibits the government from treating a group of people differently. "I was thinking: 'This is crazy, we are totally violating this law!'" Sol says. She raised her hand to ask for clarification because the teacher was using big, confusing words. "Then this kid, who had heard my presentation, looks over at me and raises his hand. 'Well, wouldn't that mean that it's not fair that gays and lesbians can't get married,' he asks. He brought it up in class! He was the last kid you'd ever expect to stand up about it."

The students in her new school elected Sol student council president and the council decided that harassment in school was a real problem. A lover of theater, Sol proposed using drama to educate peers about prejudice. Together, students created a series of skits on the many forms of harassment. They called the project SATTELITE, Students Against Totally Terrible, Explicit, Life-Altering, Ill-Mannered Teasing, Etc.

Students began the show by yelling out words of hate: fatso, fruit, schizo. They defined harassment: any mean word, look, or action that hurts a person's body, feelings, or possessions. One skit showed boys making comments about girls' bodies as they walked by. Another was about a Hmong student struggling in math. Instead of being sympathetic, other kids said: "Oh, you're Chinese, you should be good at math."

Sol knows first-hand how far we still have to go to end prejudice. "Once, I heard a white kid say a really racist comment to an African-American kid, who responded by slapping him," Sol says. "Police were called in and the African-American girl got the harshest punishment." When Sol got home she yelled and cried for an hour, saying: "Oppression feels so huge. I don't know what to do!"

But Sol's hopeful that she and other kids eventually will create powerful ways to challenge injustice. "The amazing thing about youth is that when we see something wrong in the world, we want to change it," she says. "We have this special power, this creative energy to tackle problems. We can do something about it. We believe."

WHAT YOU CAN DO
Put on a diversity play
Speak out against slurs
Do a school project on discrimination

Side by Side

Jason Dean Crowe

"We counteract hatred through acts of kindness." —Jason Crowe

On May 27, 1992, twenty-two people were massacred in a Muslim neighborhood in Sarajevo, Bosnia. Some Serbs, who wanted to rid Bosnia of people who were not Serbian, fired a mortar shell into a line of men, women, and children as they waited to buy bread.

Vedran Smailovic, a cello player, lost close neighbors in the massacre. Distraught, he carried his cello into the crater formed by the shell and played for 22 days straight, one day for each innocent victim. Bullets whistled around him, but he did not budge.

Far across the globe, in Newburg, Indiana, a 10-year-old was inspired by the cellist's bravery. "I knew right then in my spirit that I had to do something to keep the story alive and to honor the Bosnians," says Jason Crowe. His plan: commission a statue and send it to Bosnia. "I want to show the world that kids don't want genocide, we want peace and harmony," says Jason.

Killing people because of their race or ethnicity is called genocide or ethnic cleansing. Jason first became concerned about genocide when he learned about how Hitler and the Nazis slaughtered millions of Jews. "I was 8 and I read every single book I could find to try to understand what motivated Hitler to commit genocide and why the German people followed him," Jason says. No book could help him find the answer. "I really couldn't determine why he did what he did, other than he was demented."

But he couldn't dismiss the Holocaust as a fluke when the Ku Klux Klan came to town. They threw a rally ten miles from his doorstep. "It was so close to home, it made me realize how big an issue discrimination is," he says.

A Strong Symbol

Jason hopes the statue will remind people how important it is to take a stand against discrimination. Jason began the statue project by interviewing sculptors. He found one he liked, David Kocka, a peace activist. But a life-sized statue in bronze would cost a hefty $50,000. Unless Jason could get a company to ship it for free, shipping would cost another $25,000 to $50,000. "Being 10 and naive, I immediately wrote to the President to ask him for funding," he says. He got a personal reply—but no cash.

At first, Jason wanted a sculpture of the cellist to place in the spot of the massacre. But when he began raising money for the project, some kids wondered why they were being asked to donate money for a statue of a man in a tuxedo playing his cello.

Their questions forced Jason to rethink the statue. "The spirit of the Bosnian people is the spirit of multiculturalism, because the true Bosnians never gave up on their neighbors and still want to rebuild a society where all ethnic groups and religions live side by side," says Jason. He decided the new statue should capture three spirits: the spirit of multiculturalism, the spirit of harmony, and the spirit of children all over the world who want to grow up in peace.

After making a foot-high miniature, the sculptor began work on the life-sized bronze. The statue portrays five children of different ethnicities from ages 5 to 15, playing on logs in the forest and holding hands. A large space divides two logs and a child reaches across the gap to a younger child. "It's like Michelangelo's painting, where God reaches out to Adam. The children in the statute reach across the divide, bridging the gap between different ethnic, religious, and age groups," Jason says. Another child holds two sticks and pretends he's playing a violin.

Paper Chains for Peace

Jason has raised $25,000 through donations from people who have read about his project in newspapers and magazines or on his Web site. Jason believes in angels. "You can't tell who they are, but they have been put here to do the job of an angel," he says. "They just appear in someone's life, do something really good, and disappear." Jason's angel is an art collector who sent a $15,000 check for the statue.

Through his Web site, message boards, and e-mail lists, Jason has recruited kids all around the world to help raise money for the statue. Jason calls the Internet a powerful tool against discrimination. "You can connect with anyone you want," he says. "It's really heart-to-heart, because you don't have any barriers, which break down communication in real life, such as what someone looks like, what they act like, skin color, any of the stuff that leads to prejudice." Jason has appointed 15 other kids around the world to be Statue Ambassadors.

To commemorate the 10-year anniversary of the bread-line massacre and to raise money, the Statue Ambassadors are throwing Harmony in the Park. "One big, nationwide ethnic fest," Jason calls it, with places for artists to show their works, vendors to sell ethnic food, musicians to play, and kids and adults to speak out against discrimination and violence. Plans are afoot in Las Vegas, San Francisco, Boston, and other cities across the country—even in Guam!

Statue Ambassadors will also sell paper links for a Chain of Hope, from 25 cents to a dollar apiece. "We're trying to get enough links to span the United States," Jason says. "Not that we'll actually pull it across the mountains and rivers, but that we'll get it long enough that it could get across America."

Harmony in ACTion

Jason works for harmony in his

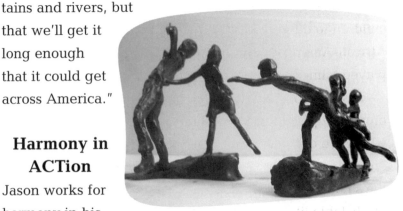

hometown, too. "My goal in life is to change people's mindsets," he says. "To change the stereotypes, change the common images, change group thinking, make people think out of the box, make people abandon the bad old ways, get people to be more open." And that includes his biggest success to date: changing the media image of youth culture.

He invited local middle and high schoolers to join YOUth for Harmony in ACTion. "We counteract hatred through acts of kindness," he says. The members come from many backgrounds: African-American, Irish, Hindu, Ukrainian, Catholic, Protestant. "When people see a diverse group of kids working together, having fun, helping the community, well, what can they say? It's kind of hard to hate people who are helping you."

The kids want to send a message without preaching. "People who are different *can* work together," says Jason. "We're the younger generation, and we are all different cultures, all different races, all different religions, and we can work together. Why can't you?"

YOUth for Harmony in ACTion began with a summer reading program for fourth and fifth grades. Every Tuesday at the library, teens spent an hour introducing younger children to different cultures. They had Japanese, Jewish, African-American, and Indian speakers, showed videos, played games, and served ethnic food.

Jason wants people to examine their attitudes about other groups. "I think people discriminate because things which are different scare you," Jason says. "And people are always different from other people. Since they aren't the same as you, they don't act like you, and they aren't predictable like you. That threatens your own well-being."

To find out for himself what other religious groups are really like, he went to an Islamic Center to learn some Arabic and study the Qu'ran. "The students, teachers, parents of students, everyone there was really kind, gentle, and humble," he says.

Jason, who is home schooled, is grateful that his parents have let him find answers to his own questions. That's the best way adults can helps kids grow, he says. "Listen to kids and don't say no when we try to do something new, different, unusual, or creative," he says. "The trying itself will produce its own yes or no. Give us help if we ask for it and believe in us. Don't give us the answers that work for you. Give us the sources and direction, but let us find our own answers that work for us. If something is the truth, we are going to discover it for ourselves."

WHAT YOU CAN DO
Raise money for the harmony statue
Talk to someone different from you
Learn about other cultures and religions

IDEAS THAT CAN CHANGE THE WORLD

"Put two people who really hate each other for their color or religion in the middle of nowhere. They will learn things about each other, and learn to cope with each other because they have to survive." **—John Jackson, age 11**

"Pride is a big part of the problem. Pride in yourself can be a good thing, but we should try to make everyone proud of people from other races. If we show people the accomplishments of people of different races, they might learn to have pride in the whole country or the whole human race." **—Logan Johnson, age 14**

"Don't judge if you don't know what it feels like to be poor, rich, white, black, brown, Asian, or gay. I think that you should not say anything if you don't know what it is like to be judged. So don't open your mouth until you have experienced the pain that others feel because of being judged." **—Lorenzo Casias, age 16**

"It must start with parents. It is the parents' job to teach their children at a young age about the negativities of discrimination, because a child is influenced more by what they hear and see from their parents than what they see on TV and hear in music." **—Lee Duran, age 17**

"First, I would try to talk to the people that discriminate against other people, and ask why they do that—what their purpose for doing that is. Then I would make every person live with a person that is different from them. I would do that so they could spend time with that person and get to know them—let them find out that we are all the same no matter where we come from."

—Nancy Sandoval, age 16

 *"Be yourself, no matter what. If you are always yourself, people will learn to accept and respect you, and you will respect yourself more, too."*

—Nicole Carlson, age 14

YOUR SOLUTION!

Chapter Eight

ALL ABOUT VOLUNTEERING

"Ideas won't keep. Something must be done about them."
—Alfred North Whitehead

Yoou have more ideas on how to solve the world's problems than could ever be covered in one book. The more you know about a problem—how big it is, who it affects, what has already been tried—the better the solution you'll create. Search the Web, read in the library, or call or e-mail organizations listed in this chapter. Talk with your parents, teachers, and other kids to find out what they know. Once you've learned about a problem, put your ideas into action by following these steps.

Follow Your Heart: Look around your neighborhood, school, and community. What are you passionate about? What would you really like to change?

Start Small: You can solve big problems, but to get started and to test your ideas, start with a piece of the problem. What part do you want to attack first?

Invite Your Friends: Don't think you have to go it alone. Friends, classmates, and family may be eager to help. Set up a meeting and invite anyone you think might be interested. Visit local organizations already working on the problem.

Raise Money: If you need cash, ask friends, family, or local businesses for donations. Or apply for a grant. You'll need to be able to describe the problem, your idea, how much money you'll need, and how the money will be spent.

Jump In: Take that big first step and pick a date for your first event and make a list of things you need to do. Write down who has agreed to do what.

Invite the Media: Television stations and newspapers might be interested in what you are doing. Call or e-mail them.

Don't Give Up: Almost all the kids in this book faced obstacles along the way. But they all say if you stick with it, you can accomplish great things!

Volunteer Organizations

People in many organizations are ready to help you make your solution happen. These groups are easy to contact, especially if you know what to request. The descriptions below tell you exactly how an organization can help you and the best way to contact them. If you have access to the Web, that's a great place to start—most have great Web sites packed with information and inspiration.

National 4-H Council
7100 Connecticut Ave.
Chevy Chase, MD 20815
(800) 368-7432
info@fourhcouncil.edu
www.fourhcouncil.edu

Join a local 4-H club to use your head, heart, hands, and health for the good of your community. You can join a livestock club that raises turkeys for the hungry, or a sewing club that makes hats and scarves for the homeless. To join a local club, find your county in the government pages of the phone book. Under "Extension" services, you'll find 4-H listed. (If there is no separate listing for 4-H, call the main Extension number.) A 4-H agent will send you an application and match you with a club. New members are invited to create their own projects if existing clubs don't suit them.

Girl Scouts of the U.S.A.
420 Fifth Ave.
New York, NY 10018
(800) 478-7248
misc@girlscouts.org
www.girlscouts.org

Join 2.7 million Girl Scouts in their efforts to make their communities stronger. All Girl Scouts do community service, ranging from cooking breakfasts for the homeless to cleaning up a favorite park. To join a troop, call the 800 number to locate your nearest Girl Scout council, or go to the Girl Scout Web site and click on "council finder." The fee for joining is $7 a year. Even if you join an established troop, you will have the freedom to decide what you want to accomplish and how to do it.

Activism 2000 Project
P.O. Box E
Kensington, MD 20895
(800) 543-7693

info@youthactivism.com
www.youthactivism.com

Who can you call every week for free advice on how to work for changes that you most care about? The Activism 2000 Project. The whole organization is devoted to helping kids speak up and pursue lasting solutions. You can request free materials, or call or e-mail describing what you want to do. Activism 2000 will put you in contact with other young people pursuing similar goals, tell you about funding sources, and give tips on how to get press coverage.

Kids Care Clubs
82 Smith Ridge Road
South Salem, NY 10590
(914) 533-1101
www.kidscare.org

Ten years ago, a group of children got together to rake a lawn for an elderly neighbor. A few weeks later, the same kids made 150 bag lunches for a soup kitchen. That was the beginning of Kids Care Clubs, a network of more than 800 clubs in all 50 states—all dedicated to kids showing how much they care by creating vol-unteer projects. Find a club near you or start your own!

Youth as Resources
1700 K St. N.W., Suite 801
Washington, D.C. 20006
(202) 466-6272, ext. 131
www.yar.org
yar@ncpc.org

YAR provides small grants to young people to design and carry out service projects that address social problems and contribute to significant community change. Call or e-mail to find a YAR program near you, or to learn how to get one started in your community.

YouthVenture
1700 N. Moore Street, Suite 2000
Arlington, VA 22209
(703) 527-4126
youthventure@ashoka.org
www.youthventure.org

Youth Venture's mission is to empower young people to create and launch their own enterprises—ranging from tutoring services and virtual radio stations to video festivals and youth diabetes support groups. Youth Venture currently runs programs on the East Coast. But they have also launched the "Virtual Venturer" program, where you are taken step-by-step through the process of successfully developing your own venture.

Youth in Action
www.teaching.com/act/

At Youth In Action, an interactive Web site, you can talk with young people from more than 80 different countries about social issues most important to you. You can also participate in surveys and sign petitions, and learn about other lobbying tools.

Do Something
423 West 55th Street, 8th Floor
New York, NY 10019
mail@dosomething.org
www.dosomething.org

Do Something has provided more than $1 million to young people to turn their ideas for a better community into action. Read on-line action guides to help you do something about a cause you care about, such as violence, drunk driving, or discrimination. Start a Do Something club in your school.

Volunteers of America, Inc.
110 S. Union St.
Alexandria, VA 22314
(703) 548-2288

www.voa.org
voa@voa.org

VOA runs volunteer projects all across the country, working with disabled people, youth, elderly, and homeless people, and on health, housing, job training issues, and more. To volunteer in a project near you, go to the Location Directory on the Web site, or call or e-mail.

Youth Service America
1101 15th Street, Suite 200
Washington, DC 20005
(202) 296-2992
www.ysa.org
info@ysa.org

Youth Service America is an alliance of more than 200 organizations dedicated to increasing opportunities for you to serve your community, your nation, and the world. Join thousands of kids across the country and the world volunteering on National Youth Service Day and Global Youth Service Day. Type your zip code into the Get Involved section of the Web site to find volunteer opportunities near you.

National Youth Leadership Council
1667 Snelling Avenue North
St. Paul, MN 55108
(651) 631-3672
www.nylc.org
nylcinfo@nylc.org

Get your school involved in the service-learning movement, where students learn academic material through service projects. Learn more through the National Youth Leadership Council, a nonprofit organization that advocates for service-learning.

Corporation for National Service (CNS)
1201 New York Ave. N.W.

Washington, DC 20525
(202) 606-5000
www.cns.gov

Through CNS, the federal government supports volunteering for people of all ages. Learn how school-based service is supported through Learn and Serve America. Search for local volunteer opportunities that welcome kids or teens through VolunteerMatch on the Web site.

Your Issue

The organizations listed below can help you make a difference in the seven areas covered in this book: education, violence, hunger, the environment, homelessness, health care, and discrimination. Call, write, or e-mail today!

EDUCATION

Sack It To You!
3938 N.W. 53rd Street
Boca Raton, FL 33496
(561) 998-7720
jamo718@aol.com

Contact Josh Marcus if you want to set up a Sack It To You! chapter in your town to provide school supplies to needy students.

FairTest
National Center for Fair and Open Testing
342 Broadway
Cambridge, MA 02139
(617) 864-4810
info@fairtest.org
www.fairtest.org

Dedicated to ending abuses, misuses, and flaws of standardized tests, FairTest offers fact sheets and information to help you organize a campaign for fair testing in your school. Check out the web site or call for a kit. FairTest will also put you in touch with other student-testing activists around the country.

Power to the Youth
615 Little Silver Point Road
Little Silver, NJ 07739
(732) 530-1128
info@youthpower.net
www.youthpower.net

Power to the Youth wants you to think about what helps you learn best, and to work to make those changes in your school. Go to the Web site for ideas to revolutionize your school and to sign up for weekly e-mailings. Or request a free School Action Guide or the flier called "10 Ways to Rock Your High School."

Education Week/Teacher Magazine
Editorial Projects in Education
Suite 100
6935 Arlington Road
Bethesda, MD 20814-5233
(800) 346-1834
www.edweek.org

Visit the Web site of Education Week and Teacher Magazine for in-depth information on almost every topic in education—from class size and testing to school safety and technology. Go to the hot topic section for the basics and search the archives to learn more.

The Public Education Network
601 13th Street, N.W.
Suite 900 North
Washington, DC 20005
(202) 628-7460
pen@publiceducation.org
www.publiceducation.org

Need money to get going on a project to improve schools in your community? Apply for a mini-grant from one of more than 60 local education funds across the country. These groups also offer advice and materials that can help you make your school better. Call, e-mail, or check the Web site to find out if there is a local foundation near you.

National PTA
330 North Wabash Avenue, Suite 2100
Chicago, IL 60611
(312) 670-6782
info@pta.org
www.pta.org

Parents, teachers, and principals at most schools gather regularly at Parent Teacher Association meetings to discuss how to make their schools better. Many PTAs welcome the ideas of students. PTAs that accept students are sometimes called Parent Teacher Student Associations. Ask your parent, teacher, or principal if you can go to a PTA meeting or contact the national office to find your local PTA.

Reduce Class Size Now
2888 Ponce de Leon Court
Gulf Shores, AL 36542
(814) 422-8207
www.reduceclasssizenow.org

Many kids interviewed for this book said they think class sizes should be smaller. Join petition-signing campaigns, referendums, and lobbying efforts afoot across the country to reduce class size. Look under "State of the States" on the Web site to learn about efforts in your state. Or call, and someone will tell you whom to contact.

VIOLENCE

Club BADDD
P.O. Box 85256

Attention: Gabriella Contreras
Tucson, AZ 85754

*Please write to request information on how to start a Club
BADDD chapter to fight violence and drug use in your school.*

Teens, Crime and the Community
National Crime Prevention Council
1000 Connecticut Avenue, N.W., 13th Floor
Washington, DC 20036
(202) 261-4161
tcc@ncpc.org
www.nationaltcc.org

*Nine out of ten kids want to do something about violence in their
community, but don't know where to begin. TCC shows you
through all kinds of projects, from designing billboards on crime,
to conducting workshops on date rape, to surveying and cleaning up your neighborhood. TCC believe that teens can take a
bite out of crime.*

Students Against Violence Everywhere (S.A.V.E.)
Center for the Prevention of School Violence
313 Chapanoke Road, Suite 140
Raleigh, North Carolina 27603
(800) 299-6054
www.ncsu.edu/cpsv/save.html

*Start a violence prevention club in your school. Call for a free
manual that describes how to involve kids in conflict manage-
ment, mediation, and community service.*

Youth in Action
Office of Juvenile Justice and Delinquency Prevention
810 Seventh Street, N.W.
Washington, DC 20531
(202) 307-5911

askjj@ncjrs.org
www.ojjdp.ncjrs.org/pubs/youthinactionsum

Use music, dance, drama, negotiation skills, and crime patrols to prevent violence in your neighborhood or school. Find out how through the OJJDP's terrific Youth in Action Bulletins written specifically for kids. Check out "Arts and Performances for Prevention," "Want To Resolve a Dispute? Try Mediation," and "Stand Up and Start a School Crime Watch!" Call, write, or e-mail for the free bulletins or read them on the Web.

The Nonviolence Web
www.nonviolence.org

Here's the place to link to dozens of state, national, and international peace organizations.

Student Pledge Against Gun Violence
112 Nevada St.
Northfield, MN 55057
(507) 645-5378
mlgrow@pledge.org
www.pledge.org

Join 2.4 million students who have taken this pledge against gun violence: "I will never bring a gun to school; I will never use a gun to settle a dispute; I will use my influence with my friends to keep them from using guns to settle disputes. My individual choices and actions, when multiplied by those of young people throughout the country, will make a difference. Together, by honoring this pledge, we can reverse the violence and grow up in safety."

HUNGER

Heifer Project International
P.O. Box 808
Little Rock, AR 72203

(800) 422-0474

www.heifer.org

Give a family a gallon of milk and they have a nutritious drink for one day. Give the family a cow and you can literally stop that family's hunger forever. That is the idea behind the Heifer Project, which donates farm animals such as cows, pigs, and goats to poor people all over the world. Raise $20 and send a family a chicken, which can provide up to 200 eggs a year. A donation of $120 buys a pig, which can give birth to 20 babies a year, each growing to 200 pounds in six months! The good doesn't stop there. Every family that gets a Heifer Project animal must donate the first offspring to another needy family. So donating one animal feeds hundreds of people.

Empty Bowls

The Imagine/Render Group

P.O. Box 167

Oxford, MI 48371

(248) 628-4842

imagineren@aol.com

www.emptybowls.net

Use your hands and your heart to organize an Empty Bowls meal to raise money to fight hunger. First, fashion and fire ceramic bowls. Then serve soup in the bowls in exchange for donations to a hunger organization of your choosing. Your guests will keep the bowls to remind them that someone's bowl is always empty. Send $5 with your name and address to receive an information packet, including suggestions on how to plan an Empty Bowls event and a logo to stamp in your bowls. You even get a tiny piece of clay from the original batch used for the first Empty Bowls meal to mix with your clay.

Fast for a World Harvest

Oxfam America

26 West Street

Boston, MA 02111

(800) 597-3278
fast@oxfamamerica.org
www.oxfamamerica.org/students

Fast for a World Harvest offers an incredible array of free materials to help you teach people about hunger and raise money to feed the hungry. Call, e-mail, write, or go to the Web site for the free "Activity Handbook," which describes how to throw a hunger banquet, hunger fast, penny competition, calendar sale, art exhibition, or Hoops for Hunger. You can even get free media kits, posters, postcards, and placemats to help publicize your event.

America's Second Harvest
35 E. Wacker Dr., #2000
Chicago, IL 60601
(800) 771-2303
www.secondharvest.org

Through a network of more than 200 food banks, America's Second Harvest distributes food to 26 million Americans each year, eight million of them children. To find a food bank near you, call or go to the volunteer section of the Web site.

The Hunger Site
www.thehungersite.com

Make a free contribution of food to hungry people by simply clicking a button on this Web site. Each day you visit the site, sponsors donate one cup of food to the World Food Program, a United Nations agency that distributes food to people in need. Approximately 200 tons of food are donated every week!

Bread for the World   50
F Street, Suite 500
Washington, DC 20001
(800) 822-7323

bread@bread.org
www.bread.org

Bread for the World is a national Christian organization that lobbies Congress on hunger issues. To learn practical tips for persuading elected officials to make ending hunger a priority, request the free 12-page booklet "What You Can Do to End Hunger." For information on hunger legislation being considered in Congress, check out the Issues and Action section of the web site. That section also gives you a really easy way to send e-mails about hunger to your Congressional representatives.

Kids Can Make a Difference
P.O. Box 54
Kittery Point, ME 03905
(207) 439-9588
kids@kidscanmakeadifference.org
www.kidscanmakeadifference.org

Kids Can Make a Difference offers a free brochure, Web site, and newsletter on hunger—and advice for kids who want to fight hunger in their communities. The free, triannual "Kids Newsletter" covers current events in the war on hunger, teaches you about the physical impacts of hunger and starvation, and explores hunger's root cause: poverty. Cruise the Web site for an on-line version of the newsletter, a hunger-facts page, and a list of ideas for beginning the war on hunger in your community. Share ideas with other hunger-fighting kids on the Bulletin Board. For advice on your local hunger project, e-mail a description of what you'd like to do and your questions about how to do it. Kids Can Make a Difference wants you to act locally: don't think of hunger worldwide, think of it in your own community.

THE ENVIRONMENT

Adopt-A-Stream Foundation
Northwest Stream Center
600 128th Street, S.E.

Everett, WA 98208
(425) 316-8592
aasf@streamkeeper.org
www.streamkeeper.org

*Clean up and protect your favorite stream. Request the free
brochure, "The Five Steps to Stream Adoption," or look on the
Web site under "Streamkeeper Tools." The Adopt-A-Stream
Foundation will help you to write a plan of action complete with
short- and long-term goals for keeping your stream clean.
Adopting a stream isn't easy—you'll need to get everyone in the
watershed involved. But the rewards to you and the ecosystem
can be great!*

20/20 Vision
1828 Jefferson Place N.W.
Washington, DC 20036
(202) 833-2020
vision@2020vision.org
www.2020vision.org

*Send the president, members of congress, and the media your
thoughts on environmental issues. Go to "Take Action" on the
Web site to learn what environmental issues your lawmakers are
debating—then e-mail them your ideas.*

Earth Force
1908 Mount Vernon
Second Floor
Alexandria, VA 22301
(703) 299-9400
earthforce@earthforce.org
www.earthforce.org

*Lead local environmental campaigns created by kids for kids. Go
to the "Resource" section of the Web site to learn how to help
make your community more bike-friendly. Call or e-mail to get
involved in the latest campaign.*

National Resources Defense Council
40 West 20th Street
New York, NY 10011
(212) 727-2700
nrdcinfo@nrdc.org
www.nrdc.org

Get your facts here! While not specifically designed for kids, the NRDC Web site has amazing, easy-to-read information on clean air and water, energy, global warming, fish and wildlife, and other environmental topics. Check out the stunning photos, fascinating facts, and practical ideas on how to defend our natural resources.

Earth Day Network
811 First Avenue, Suite 454
Seattle, WA 98104
www.earthday.net

Every year on April 22nd, millions of people—young and old— celebrate the Earth and raise awareness of environmental issues through Earth Day activities. In 2001, students in Los Angeles formed a massive aerial message telling the world that it's time to "Go Solar." Join an Earth Day event in your area or throw your own. Sign up for a witty daily or weekly e-mail newsletter called Grist.

HOMELESSNESS

Habitat for Humanity
121 Habitat St.
Americus, GA 31709
(229) 924-6935
publicinfo@habitat.org
www.habitat.org

Habitat volunteers have built more than 100,000 houses in more than 79 countries, including 30,000 in the United States. Though youth under the age of 16 are not allowed to work on construc-

tion sites because of child labor laws, Habitat offers other ways for you to get involved. You can build window boxes, bird houses, or picnic tables as a housewarming gift or fundraiser; organize and serve meals to builders—even paint doors and baseboards off site. Contact Habitat to find out which of its 1,900 affiliates is nearest you.

National Coalition for the Homeless
1012 Fourteenth Street, N.W., Suite 600
Washington, DC 20005
(202) 737-6444
info@nationalhomeless.org
www.nationalhomeless.org

NCH has an ambitious mission: to end homelessness. Go to the Web site to educate yourself about homelessness and to join one of their campaigns, such as the Kids' Day on Capitol Hill. The Kids' Corner section of the Web site lists surprising facts about homelessness and describes what kids around the country are doing to stop it.

U.S. Department of Housing and Urban Development
451 7th Street, S.W.
Washington, DC 20410
(202) 708-1112
www.hud.gov/homeless

As the federal agency responsible for housing, HUD offers information and ideas on how to help the homeless. Check out the Kids Can Help the Homeless section of the Web site. Interested in volunteering at a shelter? Type your zip code, state, or city and state into the Web site to get a list of shelters near you.

YouthBuild Coalition
58 Day Street
P.O. Box 440322
Somerville, MA 02144
(617) 623-9900

ybinfo@youthbuild.org
www.youthbuild.org

*YouthBuild aims to solve three problems at once—unemploy-
ment, homelessness, and urban decay—by training unemployed
young people to renovate run-down government-owned buildings to house the homeless. Since 1993, YouthBuild students
have built or reconstructed more than 7,000 units of affordable
housing. Call, e-mail, or go to the Web site to find out how you
can support the YouthBuild Coalition.*

National Student Campaign Against Hunger and Homelessness
233 N. Pleasant Ave.
Amherst, MA 01002
(800) 664-8647
nscah@aol.com
www.nscahh.org

*NSCAHH is the largest student network in the country fighting
hunger and homelessness, with more than 600 chapters on college campuses in 45 states. Even if you are not in college yet,
students at a local chapter can help you get involved. Call or
check the Web site to find a chapter you.*

National Alliance to End Homelessness
1518 K Street, N.W., Suite 206
Washington, DC 20005
(202) 638-1526
naeh@naeh.org
www.naeh.org

*Call or check out the Web site for NAEH's great fact sheets for
kids, written especially for middle and high school students. You
can also call with specific questions about homelessness and
about how you can help.*

HEALTH CARE

Locks of Love
1640 S. Congress Ave., Suite 104
Palm Springs, FL 33461
(561) 963-1677
www.locksoflove.org

Donate your hair to make a wig for a child with medical hair loss. Donated hair must be at least 10 inches long, free from dye or perms or styling products, and clean and dry. The hair should be bundled in a ponytail or braid, placed in a plastic bag, and mailed to Locks of Love in a padded envelope with your name and address. If you want to run a hair drive, call or go to the Web site to register.

Coalition on Donation
1100 Boulders Parkway, Suite 700
Richmond, VA 23225
(804) 330-8620
coalition@shareyourlife.org
www.shareyourlife.org

By becoming an organ donor, you can save the lives of eight people and improve the lives of 50 more. Learn about organ and tissue donation and how to become a donor. Call or e-mail for a free brochure, or get everything you need on the Web site.

Junior American Red Cross
431 18th St., N.W.
Washington, DC 20006
(800) 435-7669
info@usa.redcross.org
www.redcross.org

Forty percent of Red Cross volunteers are under the age of 24. The Red Cross trains young people in all areas of disaster services, including community education, local preparation, and disaster response through Red Cross disaster action teams and youth disaster corps. On the Web, go to the Youth section. Or call to find out how to get involved.

World Health Organization (WHO)
www.who.org

Though not written specifically for young people, the World Health Organization's summaries of health topics from A to Z, found on their Web site, are an incredible source of information on health issues from asthma and air quality to vaccinations.

Jump Rope for Heart
Hoops for Heart
American Heart Association
7272 Greenville Avenue
Dallas, TX 75231
(800) 242-8721
www.americanheart.org

Jump rope or play basketball for your own fitness and to raise money for the American Heart Association. Call or visit the Web site to find participating schools or to organize an event at your school.

DISCRIMINATION

Arrest the Racism: Racial Profiling in America
American Civil Liberties Union
125 Broad Street, 18th Floor
New York, NY 10004
www.aclu.org/profiling/

Read real stories about racial profiling and studies on how com-mon it is, and learn about current court cases and legislation, at the ACLU's Web site. If you believe you have been stopped by police because of your race, report it to the ACLU. You can also send a fax to your members of Congress through the site.

The Cello Cries On
P.O. Box 441
Newburgh, IN 47629
jdc@sigecom.net
www.peaceinc.org/networking/cellocries/cellocries.htm

For more information about Jason Crowe's Children's
International Peace & Harmony Statue, Harmony in the Park,
and YOUth for Harmony in ACTion, check out his Web site or
send him an e-mail.

COLAGE
Children of Lesbians and Gays Everywhere
3543 18th Street, Number 1
San Francisco, CA 94110
(415) 861-5437
colage@colage.org
www.colage.org

COLAGE offers support to the eight million sons and daughters
of gay and lesbian parents in the United States. Log on to the
Web site to find a COLAGE chapter near you, for volunteer
opportunities, statistics—even answers to questions about having
gay or lesbian parents.

Seeking Harmony in Neighborhoods Everyday (ShiNE)
648 Broadway, Suite 301
New York, NY 10012
(877) 744-6365
info@shinemail.org
www.shine.com

ShiNE is a national organization that uses art, music, technology,
and sports to engage and empower young people to take a
stand, use their voices, and impact their world. In addition to
helping you start a local club, ShiNE offers grant money to
young people who want to promote social harmony in their
schools and communities.

162

Positive-Youth Foundation
P.O. Box 64
Greencastle, PA 17225
(717) 597-9065
attitude@epix.net
www.positive-youthfoundation.org

This group strives to educate young people about racism through music and entertainment. Visit the web site to learn how to start an anti-racist, unity, or multicultural club, how to host a benefit concert to raise money for an anti-racist project in your community, or how to set up a table at a concert someone else puts on.

United Against Hate
www.unitedagainsthate.org

Visit the Web site to learn about legislation proposed to punish acts of violence against people based on their race, color, religion, national origin, gender, sexual orientation, or disability.

Awards

Winning an award can bring attention, and sometimes money, to your cause. Apply yourself—or nominate your favorite kid activist!

The Prudential Spirit of the Community Awards
The Prudential Insurance Company
751 Broad Street
Newark, NJ 07102
(888) 450-9961
www.prudential.com

Many of the young people described in this book are Prudential honorees. Maybe you can become one, too! Every year since 1996, Prudential has recognized one middle school and one high school student from each state, and awarded each of the top ten youth volunteers in the country $5,000, a gold medallion, and a trophy. To get an application, call, write, or download one from the Web site. Applications are due to your school principal, Girl Scout council executive director, or county 4-H agent no later than the last weekday in October.

The Kids Hall of Fame
Three Ibsen Court
Dix Hills, NY 11746
(631) 242-9105
www.thekidshalloffame.com

Get your face on a trading card! The Kids Hall of Fame publishes inspirational stories of people under the age of 20 on its trading cards and Web site, and in its magazine. Call or check out the Web site to learn how to apply.

National Caring Awards
Caring Institute
228 7th Street, SE
Washington, DC 20003
www.caringinstitute.org

The Caring Institute honors the activities of Americans who ennoble the human race by helping others. Every year, five junior and senior high school students are selected from nominations submitted by their school principals. Winners receive a college scholarship. Nomination forms are available on the Web site.

Start Something Awards
33 South Sixth Street
P.O. Box 1392
Minneapolis, MN 55440
(800) 316-6142
www.startsomething.target.com

Target and the Tiger Woods Foundation have teamed up to offer kids 11 to 14 years old a step-by-step program to help you reach *your dreams and become a role model. After completing a series of activities, you'll be eligible to win scholarships ranging from $100 to $10,000. Enroll on-line or pick up a brochure at the Target store nearest you.*

President's Student Service Awards
P.O. Box 189
Wilmington, DE 18990
(866) 550-7772
pssa.info@verizon.net
www.student-service-awards.org

More than 70,000 young people have been recognized with these awards for their work to improve their communities. All students from kindergarten through college who contribute at least 100 hours of service a year are eligible for the Gold Award. Winners receive a pin and a certificate. Scholarships are also available.

International Youth Hall of Fame
300 Queen Anne Avenue North, #201
Seattle, Washington 98109
(206) 623-6770
youthhall@msn.org
www.youthhall.org

Unlike other traditional recognition programs, IYHF is not a competition. Instead, communities that have chapters encourage everyone—families, friends, neighbors, schools, service clubs, religious institutions, businesses, government agencies, and non-profit organizations—to notice the positive efforts of their youth and nominate them for recognition. Nominees decide if they want to be honored by publicly taking a pledge to mentor and encourage another young person, and then partner with them in a community service project. Upon completion of their project, they become officially an honoree and get to create a personal message hand-etched into ceramic tiles for one of the Youth Walls of Fame.

The Giraffe Project
197 Second St.
P.O. Box 759
Langley, WA 98260
(360) 221-7989
office@giraffe.org
www.giraffe.org

Your story could inspire others. The Giraffe Project wants to hear about young people who stick their necks out for the good of others. The Giraffe Project has been finding these heroes and commending them as "Giraffes" since 1982. The project tells the stories of Giraffes in the media, from podiums, and in schools, inspiring others to stick their necks out. Contact the Giraffe Project with your story of selfless service to others.

Sources

CHAPTER 1: You Know School
BIC Corporation
Harper's Magazine
U.S. Department of Education
U.S. Department of Justice
U.S. General Accounting Office
*Getting By: What American Teenagers Really Think About Their
      Schools.* New York: Public Agenda, 1997.
FairTest

CHAPTER 2: Give Peace A Chance
The Brady Campaign
Center for Media and Public
Children's Defense Fund
FBI
Harper's Magazine
National Association of School Psychologists
National Crime Victimization Survey for 1999, Bureau of Justice
      Statistics
U.S. Centers for Disease Control and Prevention

CHAPTER 3: The World's Table
Bread for the World
Church World Service
Kempf, Stephanie. *Finding Solution to Hunger: A sourcebook for
      middle and upper school teachers.* New York: Kids Can
      Make A Difference, 1997.
Food First
Harper's Magazine
Oxfam America
Second Harvest
UNICEF
U.S. Department of Agriculture

CHAPTER 4: Your Planet
E Patrol Foundation, Sprint
Gutnik, Martin J. *Experiments that Explore Recycling.*
      Brookfield, CT: The Milbrook Press, 1992.
Javna, John. *50 Simple Things Kids Can Do to Recycle.*
      Berkeley: Earth Works Press, 1994.
U.S. Environmental Protection Agency

CHAPTER 5: A Place to Call Your Own
National Coalition for the Homeless
U.S. Department of Housing and Urban Development

CHAPTER 6: Get Well Soon
Bill & Melinda Gates Foundation
Duke University Medical School
Institute of HeartMath
Johns Hopkins School of Medicine
Oxfam America
U.S. Census Bureau

CHAPTER 7: The Face Of Fairness
Jane Elliott
Peters, William. *A Class Divided, Then and Now.* New Haven:
    Yale University Press, 1987.

Acknowledgments

I want to thank the young people whose stories and words grace these pages. You are the foundation of this book and the promise of a better world.

Thanks also go to my readers, editors, agent, and assistants: Ellie Caldwell, Lisa Cohn, Nora E. Coon, J. Piper Gallucci, Alex Galt, Bonni Goldberg, Barbara Mann, Michelle McCann, Sue Moshofsky, Andy Murray, Ron Norman, Catherine Paglin, Meredith Phelan, Travis Shields, Sarah Thomas, Kristin Walrod, Kathleen Younkin, Nichola Zaklan, and the students of Irvington Elementary and Fernwood Middle School. Your efforts and suggestions have made this a better book. Special thanks to Prudential for identifying and celebrating the efforts of so many young people across the country.

Finally, I want to thank the Schulz and Russman families, and my husband, Craig, and son, Cobi. You have taught me the strongest solution to the world's problems—love.

About the Author

Elizabeth Rusch has been hanging out with kids and writing about them for more than a dozen years. Her writing for children and teens has been published in *Read, Know Your World Extra*, and *Istash.com*. As a Contributing Editor to *Child*, a national newsstand magazine read by more than a million parents, Rusch interviewed students around the country for a monthly column called "KidSpeak." Rusch also contributes regular articles to *The Oregonian*, the largest daily newspaper in the Northwest. Her award-winning writing on education, parenting, health, travel, and the outdoors has also been published in *Parents, American Baby, Parenting, Family Life, Fit Pregnancy, Woman's Day, Ladies' Home Journal, Family Circle, Backpacker, Beliefnet.com*, and *Zooba.com*, among others.

Rusch is the former Managing Editor of *Teacher Magazine*, a national magazine for elementary and secondary schoolteachers. She lives in Portland, Oregon, with her husband, Craig, and her son, Cobi.

For discussion questions, to share ideas with other kids, and to find volunteer opportunities near you, visit **www.generationfix.com**.